Miracle at the Foundry

Toby Campbell

Miracle at the Foundry
by Toby Campbell

Story copyright owned by Tyree Campbell
Cover illustration "Of the Light" by t.santitoro

First Printing, August 2024

Published by Into The Light Books

Into The Light Books is an imprint of Hiraeth Publishing and is devoted to publishing works of a religious nature.

Hiraeth Publishing
P.O. Box 1248
Tularosa, NM 88352
e-mail: hiraethsubs@yahoo.com

Visit www.hiraethsffh.com for online science fiction, fantasy, horror, scifaiku, and more. Stop by our online bookstore for novels, magazines, anthologies, and collections. **Support the small, independent press...and your First Amendment rights.**

For God: my gift to Him, as is everything else that I do.

For Father Patrick Montgomery, pastor of Our Lady of the Light in La Luz, New Mexico, who with God's guidance helped me get back on my feet.

001

The office where I work part-time looks unassuming. It's located in a suburban strip mall in The City, almost lost between a hair salon and an Italian restaurant, more hole-in-the-wall than office. Appointed with a single wooden desk of pine, a swivel chair, a filing cabinet, a laptop with a printer and fax, a small table with a coffeemaker and three unmatched ceramic mugs, and a stuffed chair for the client, all illuminated by glowing panels in the ceiling, its walls retain the color of the previous occupant, a tax accountant. Which means gray walls, an off-white ceiling, and cheap speckled linoleum on the floor. The front door is the only way in or out—behind the rear wall, where the back door might have been, is a cubbyhole room inaccessible from our side, where the restaurant keeps its trash until pickups on Mondays and Thursdays. To the right of the door, as you are looking in from the street, is a window, and above the window is painted in soft, deep blue block letters: Anthony Lost Foundry.

The name is misleading, of course. In a true foundry, various metals are beaten into useful shapes. Under the sign, ideally, there should be in smaller letters: You Lose It, We Find It. But Mister Lost—Anthony, but never ever Tony—has yet to paint those letters.

FWIW, my name is Eric McCleod, I'm twenty, and working my way through college. I attend The City University, where I major in History and Sociology. Working for the Foundry pays for the studio apartment I rent a few blocks away, and the food I consume there, and the customary incidentals. I suppose I am an acolyte, in that I help Anthony in his work, and that relationship occasionally takes on a religious tone. Outsiders might call it magic, what he does. I know better.

Let me give you an example. A week ago, a lady entered the shop looking for help in finding her house keys. She had looked everywhere. In her purse, her pockets, the sofa, the stuffed chair, the kitchen and bathroom counters, the desk and its drawers, the jewelry box—and as she listed each location for Anthony, she grew more frustrated and vocal. He met her eyes evenly, and listened patiently. He claims this is a bonding process. A person who knows absolutely that he or she is being listened to, with rapt attention, is far more likely to expand what is being said, thereby imparting information that is likely to lead to a solution. So he listened, and the very act of listening seemed to bring calm to her. When she had finished, he asked just one question.

"On the day you noticed your keys missing, had you gone out shopping?"

She admitted as much.

At that point Anthony closed his eyes. His lips moved, as if in a silent prayer. When he opened his eyes again, perhaps a minute had passed. He told her, "You will find your keys in one of two places: the car ignition, or the front door lock." He then instructed me to accompany her, verify the finding of the keys, and collect the modest fee.

Some folks say he's not really praying. I know better. More than once I'd wondered whether he wasn't God Himself. But I soon dismissed that notion, for I was unable to fathom why God would be running a lost-and-found. Not that He couldn't, but...well...ineffable are His ways.

On this particular Monday morning, I arrived after my class in Medieval History to find a client already in the office. She looked up as I entered—the office is the sort of place where you think you're the only one in it. In her early twenties, and wearing a simple cotton frock bordered with small blue flowers, she had long brown hair tied in a ponytail and stuffed down the back of the frock. Holding a coffee mug—the one on which was painted a saint holding a bird on his index finger—she briefly regarded me with intense blue eyes before returning her attention to Anthony.

"My assistant, Eric," he said. "Eric, this is Miss Leah Hawthorne. Now that you're here, I'd like you to listen in."

Hawthorne turned in the chair and extended a hand to me, which I took for a few seconds. The motion had made the hem of her frock ride up a little past her knees. She had very good legs (hey, I'm a twenty-year-old young man, I notice things like that). With no place to sit down, I veered off to one side, near the wall, and stood rather behind her to avoid further distraction.

A little nod from Anthony bade her continue.

She seemed reluctant to speak, and for a moment I thought Anthony would ask me to leave. But her hesitation stemmed from not quite knowing how to address the problem of her lost item. Evidently she had just arrived, and had been eased to coffee and a chair and a short introduction.

"It's difficult to explain," she began. Her contralto held just a touch of smoke. "I'm...I feel lost. I'm not sure who I am, or what I am to do. I've felt this way for...for years, I think. I don't know why. Sometimes, I'll stop—in the middle of doing dishes, or during a lecture in class, or even on a sidewalk. One time I was just window shopping at a mall, with nothing special going on with me, and I just...oh, God, I just went blank. What am I doing here? What am I looking for? Who am I? I know it sounds silly, but I—"

Anthony shook his head. "It's not silly at all to think of finding yourself," he assured her. "Or to wonder about yourself and your purpose."

She seemed to take some solace from that. "I've tried therapy. The last therapist I saw suggested that, as I was only twenty, I would grow out of this uncertainty and find my way." She added, with slight bitterness, "For that, I could have saved myself a hundred and twenty-five dollars. I-I...Mister Lost, you're—"

"Anthony," he said. "Please."

Accepting, she inclined her head. "Anthony, you're kind of my last resort."

He smiled that smile. "I usually am."

Once again she hesitated. "Is this...search something you can...do?"

"It is rather different," he told her, his tone as always gentle. "Usually I am asked to locate an object or, sometimes, another person. But I accept your case. And Leah? I have never failed."

"But it might take some time," she put in. A palpable relief washed over her. "Yes, I understand that. But you will help me?"

"Yes, I will. But I do want to consider what you've told me before I decide on a plan of action. I have your cell number."

Hawthorne gave a light laugh. "Sometimes I feel as if I'm in a cell."

"I can imagine. Leah, I'll make contact with you tomorrow afternoon, and give you something to do. In the meantime...have you had anything to eat this morning?"

She placed her free hand on her stomach and shook her head.

For the first time during the interview, Anthony looked at me.

"You still have that card I gave you? Good. Please take Leah to breakfast. I recommend the *Waffle World* just down the street. Leah, you took the bus here? Eric, when breakfast is done, accompany her back to her apartment or to the university, then return here."

Uncertainty filled Leah's blue eyes as she stood up. Maybe my smile helped. I held the door for her, and we hit the sidewalk.

Sunlight made Leah's hair glisten. I told myself to stop noticing things like that. Eyes straight ahead, and never mind that as we walked side by side my hand inadvertently (I swear) brushed against hers once or twice. I found myself wondering what she was thinking. We kept to a reasonably brisk pace, not speaking to one another, and reached the entrance to *Waffle World* in about ten minutes. Again I held the door for her. Greeting us was a bubbly young woman in a brown-and-yellow striped uniform meant to represent maple syrup and butter. She led us to a booth by the front window. Leah and I sat down on opposite sides of the table.

While I fumbled for something to say, the food server arrived with menus and glasses of ice water, then stood in anticipation, pen poised over a notepad. I looked to Leah.

She did not bother with the menu. "A waffle, please," she said. "And sausage links. A soda to drink."

That sounded good. "The same for me," I said.

The server wrote this down, and hurried off.

Now Leah looked directly at me. "Am I, you know, supposed to talk to you about this? To tell you things?"

I shook my head. "Whatever you want to talk about is fine with me. Or not talk at all. Some folks prefer silence while they eat."

"No, I meant…about my…case."

"Anything you want." I gave her a nudge. "May I call you Leah?" She nodded. "I'm Eric. What are you studying at the university?"

"First-year courses," she answered, readily enough. "Humanities, English Comp, Algebra." She hesitated, as if there were another subject, but she thought better of revealing it.

That she listed Humanities first was significant. I said, "Doctor Lowell?"

"Yes. Do you know him?"

"I had Humanities last year. He gave me a B. But maybe I learned enough for an A later on."

"You're a second-year student? But you look...how old are you?" A beat passed. "If I may ask," she added.

"Same as you: twenty."

"You look younger."

"You look older."

And she smiled for the first time. "Is that a good thing?"

I shrugged. "It's part of who you are, Leah."

Breakfast arrived. We sat back while the plates and syrups were placed before us. The server had the usual comment—if we needed anything else, just let her know. The waffles had been done to a nicely brown turn, and among the syrup rack was a beaker of real maple. We both looked at it, but she reached it first.

"Like at home," she said, pouring. "My brother always got it before I could. This time, I win."

Anthony says the key is to listen. Everything she said to me, I filed away.

"He's older, your brother?"

She said yes around a mouthful of sausage, but her face had saddened, and a touch of moisture filmed her eyes. I wondered whether I had stumbled into the wrong question. But she continued, readily enough.

"He, Micah, joined the Army," she told me. "I wished he hadn't, but...well, he, he was killed in Afghanistan."

"I'm sorry." It always seems banal to say that when informed that someone died or was killed, but I have no idea what to say otherwise.

"Yeah. So was I." She began to address the waffle, slapping pats of butter on it, and dousing it with the syrup again. Presently she made a face, and glared at the beaker in her hand. "But I already put syrup on this," she groaned. "Oh, I don't know what I'm doing."

"Trade with me," I said, pushing my plate toward her.

She blinked. "What? Are you...are you sure?"

"I just got out of Medieval History," I told her. "I can use the sugar high."

She laughed, and we traded. She had eaten all three of her links, while I had yet to touch mine. She offered them back to me, but I declined.

"They're already on your side of the table," I said. "Returning will only confuse them."

She considered that. "Sometimes I feel like these links, then. Not knowing where I'm going."

"You mean, with your life."

"Yes. Yes! That's it, exactly. I'm a wandering sausage link."

"Well, now that we have you identified..."

After bestowing a smile on that, she drew a long breath and sighed, and fell to eating silently. Minutes passed. I finished the waffle and half the soda. She was chewing thoughtfully. Without warning, she blurted, "Micah chose the Army. He...he made a bad choice, and it killed him. Eric, I don't want to make a bad choice."

"Thus your sense of being lost," I said gently. "Of not having a purpose to give you an identity."

Leah dropped the fork onto the plate and sat back. Unfocused blue eyes gazed at me, through me, through the back of the booth, through the window, and on out into the universe itself. I had no idea where she was; neither did she, probably. But something had shined a light into her.

It took Leah a good five minutes to come back to the present moment and to resume eating. She said nothing, as if she did not know what to say, or was afraid to say it.

I stabbed the fork into a bite of waffle. "It's not too bad," I said. "A bit mapley."

She set her fork down, and gazed at me as if wondering who I was and what I was doing there. But her eyes took only a few seconds to come back into focus.

"I'm being very mysterious, aren't I?" she asked.

"Tucked into an enigma, wrapped up as a conundrum, and shipped via UPS as a dilemma." A little laugh escaped me. "No, Leah, I think you are what you have described yourself to be. The task of Anthony Lost Foundry is to help you find your identity. For Anthony to do that, it helps to know as much of the story as possible."

Her lips tightened. "That means you will tell him of our talk here."

So I broke a rule. "Aside from mentioning your excessive use of maple syrup, no, Leah. I don't have to, and I won't if that should be your wish. But it would be helpful if you would tell Anthony what you have told me."

"But...but to what end?"

"We won't know that until you tell him what you told me."

Leah slid from the bench and got to her feet. "Will you pay the check?"

"Yes, of course, but—"

"There's no need to see me back," she said, insistent. "I'll wait for his call tomorrow." And she walked out of the restaurant without so much as a glance back.

002

Cultural Anthropology kept me from returning to the Foundry until two-thirty, at which time Anthony was listening to another client. I stood discreetly by, making yet another mental note to bring a folding metal chair to the office. He did not introduce me, which meant he wanted me to listen unobtrusively. The woman had misplaced a ring that held considerable sentimental value for her.

Thumping against the rear wall of the office interrupted what she was saying. Anthony lifted his eyes in a brief despair, a what-can-you-do expression on his face. Presently the thumping stopped, the trash and garbage on the other side having been dumped.

"The restaurant next door has a dish-cleaning alcove that's right behind our office," he explained, for maybe the thirtieth time in the year I've been working here.

The woman seemed to pay it no mind. She was the sort who would have an heirloom ring, and wear it for special occasions. In her late forties, I guessed, though I had been wrong about Leah's age, and wearing a white blouse and brown tweed skirt that might have been in fashion fifteen years earlier, in England. She had bound up her graying black hair in what I believe is called a chignon, but had missed a few wisps. An aroma of money hovered over her. I thought I might have seen her at Mass at Our Lady of the Light, but wasn't certain. In any event, I had been excluded from the interview.

But I knew what Anthony would say, eventually; I'd heard this sort of story before. When she had finished, he closed his eyes as usual, and his lips moved. It's not an act, like I had thought on my first day in the office. I think he really does pray for guidance. Sometimes I wish I had that kind of faith; I'm working on it, but there's so much—and yet in some ways so little—to accept and understand.

Opening his eyes, he said, "Mrs. Cordwainer, a ring like that is usually worn on special occasions. Otherwise, it is kept in a jewelry box or a special box or drawer. You've looked there, so we can eliminate that as a possibility. In such circumstances, I often find that a break in routine can account for the location of the object. You do something absently, not thinking about it because your mind is elsewhere. You've searched the counters, the bathroom, and so on. What you did not check was the soap dish in the bathroom where you washed your hands after...afterwards. Try there."

Cordwainer was aghast. "Oh, my God, you're right!" she exclaimed. "Now I remember taking it off and putting it in the dish. The phone had just rung, and I was hurrying...oh, thank you! I *know* it's there, under the bar of soap." She got to her feet and shouldered her purse. "Oh, I am going to tell everyone about you," she said, as she laid a check on his desk. "Everyone!"

Anthony stood up, shook her hand, and invoked a, "Bless you. And good luck."

After the door had closed behind her, he said, "I assume you had a general talk with Leah Hawthorne."

I dropped onto the stuffed chair. "A difficulty arose," I said. "Aside from one minor incident," here I told him about the double syrup, "I promised not to divulge what she told me. I did recommend that she tell you herself. And...she left abruptly, and did not wish for me to see her home or to class, wherever she was bound."

He considered this, and I knew from his expression that he understood. "Without going into detail, what was your overall impression?" he asked me.

I had to choose my words carefully. "Let's just say that, based on what she told you and me during the interview, she might have been...easing back on the truth a little."

Anthony folded his hands together and laid them on the desktop. "Something in the family," he said. It was not a question, nor did I respond. He understood that as well. "Something has frightened her into uncertainty," he went on, musing, not addressing me directly. "Very well. I told her I would call her tomorrow. We'll keep to that schedule." He picked up the check and laid it in the desk drawer.

We spent the next hour reading: he from an encyclical—I couldn't see which one—and me from the chemistry textbook, for I had lab the next day. At four it became apparent that no one else had lost anything, and he bade me good luck with my lab, with a friendly admonition not to blow up anything. Rather than walk, I caught the Number 17 bus just outside, which let me out a block from my studio apartment.

The apartment is simple and comfortable and—best of all—affordable. It is located in the attic of a long building; it used to be a dance studio, but that went out of business, so it was partitioned off into half a dozen studio apartments, rented for nominal fees and mostly to university students. Mine is the middle one of three along the front of the building, so I have a view of the street two floors down and the park on the other side.

Dinner was a decent grade of miso ramen, some cream cheese on crackers, and a glass of milk. I had other culinary options, but I was not very hungry. Textbooks beckoned, as did the thought of a movie on my DVD screen. I laid back on the bed, head nestled on the pillow, fingers laced behind my neck. And thought about Leah Hawthorne instead, of course.

That musing did not go very far, interrupted as it was by some loud grumbling next door (yes, the walls are thin). As that apartment belonged to Benj Davis, one of my best friends, I got up and went to knock on his door.

Despite the short ponytail in back, his black hair was in disarray when he answered the door. His long face was distraught. His white tee shirt was only partially tucked in, and the leather belt holding up his blue jeans was askew. He invited me in readily enough, but it was clear that something had him distracted. He raised his arms and cracked his knuckles on the ceiling—like me, he's six-two, and the ceilings are low. He emitted a low growl, and then apologized.

"Did you lose something?" I asked.

Gray eyes widened, staring at me. "How did you know?"

"Hey, it's a conversation opener. You sounded distressed."

He sighed. "Those thin walls. I didn't mean to disturb you." He flopped down on a stuffed chair he had rescued from an easement in a residential neighborhood and covered with a white sheet. "I was balancing my checkbook on the lappie," he told me. "I bought some groceries, and I now can't find the receipt."

"And you're close to overdrawn again."

He shot me a worried look. "I don't know if I can make the rent this month. And *Pens & Paper* is thinking of cutting back on hours."

I perched on a corner of his desk. "You can bank online, right? Just call up the account and see—"

He shook his head. "It wasn't posted. I bought the groceries earlier this evening. It won't be posted until tomorrow morning."

"Surely you can estimate."

"Yeah, but..."

My brow bunched. "You're *that* close to overdrawn?"

Benj was on the verge of tears.

"Right, then," I said. "You checked the grocery bags?"

A nod.

"You paid with a debit card? Sometimes the cashier will wrap the card in the receipt. Did you look in your wallet?"

Another nod.

"Pockets?"

"It's no use," Benj moaned.

I gave his desktop a once-over. Like mine, his was cluttered, but I saw nothing that resembled a receipt. "You put the groceries away, right? What about the counters?"

He shook his head.

"Benj, what's your habit with receipts?" I asked. "Do you always do the same thing?"

He heaved a weary sigh. "Most of the time, it goes into one of the bags."

"So this time you broke the habit, for some reason."

He admitted as much. "The girl who bagged the groceries was kinda cute. But I don't see...I don't know what I did with the receipt."

"Saint Anthony, come around," I intoned. "Something's lost, and got to be found."

Benj stared up at me. "A prayer?"

"Of a sort. More like a mantra."

"I don't think it's helping."

"Let's review," I suggested. "You went shopping."

"Yes."

"You came straight home."

"Yes."

"You went shopping dressed like that."

"Well, no, I..." Abruptly he stood up and dashed to the bedroom. A moment later he emerged, brandishing the receipt in his hand. "It was in the pocket of my jersey," he shouted. He aimed for the desk, and I disembarked from the corner. "Sixteen dollars and forty-nine cents. I can pay the rent!"

"Good to know."

He sobered. "Thank you."

"Any time."

He headed for the kitchen. "Want a soda?"

"No, I've got chem lab tomorrow."

"Don't blow up anything."

I waved him goodbye and left.

Back in my own place, I thought about what I had just done. The process seemed so natural, yet I knew it had been heavily influenced by Anthony. The year I'd worked for him had rubbed off. And I had no doubt that the mantra had been answered. No proof of that, just a feeling of certainty. Maybe that came with the territory of success.

I had not considered myself religious when I started working for him. Mass most Sundays was the extent of my activity. I did not consider myself religious now. And yet. And yet.

I said a silent thanks to Saint Anthony, and cracked open the textbook.

The chemistry laboratory remained intact after my titrations and several deft applications of a Bunsen burner. Noon arrived as class was dismissed. I walked with a cluster of students to the Student Union and had lunch and some conversation. Gwendy Paris had removed a stopper without thinking, and had spilled a blue titrate all over the counter. A slight young woman with short golden hair, she hunched her shoulders and cringed while others laughed, but she bore up well under the comments at her expense. I patted her on the arm to console her, and she found a smile for me. As I looked past her shoulder, I caught a glimpse of someone familiar: Leah Hawthorne. She was headed for the exit and, presumably, the bus stop. I thought of catching her up, but had no idea what I would say to her if I did so.

Because it was only a glimpse, I was not certain that it was Leah. Her back was to me. She was wearing, not a frock, but black jeans and a green pullover. Still, it was a reminder that I might see her around the campus.

Gwendy tagged my arm and said I had three minutes to catch my own bus, which put an end to any further conversation. But there was a touch of gratitude in her green, gold-flecked eyes.

Anthony was the office's only occupant by the time I arrived. He was in the middle of reading news articles on his laptop, and he was scowling. I looked a question at him and he shook his head: no clients so far today. Sometimes I wonder how he stays in business. He charges a modest fee, always the same: twenty-five dollars. In a good week, by my unofficial estimate, he might take in a couple hundred dollars, which would not even pay the office rent. His finances were none of my business, of course, and he always paid me on time. But I could not help wondering about his other sources of revenue.

He stocked a few magazines on a corner shelf, and I took the top one, a recent issue of *Biblical Archeology Review*. It features articles about archeological digs at locations mentioned in the Bible. This issue contained information about a wellspring of fresh water in eastern Jerusalem, in an area known as the Millo, that had been flowing since around 1100 B.C. A tunnel had been excavated back then, leading from the springs into western Jerusalem, to provide water there, especially in times of war or siege. Another article in an earlier issue of *BAR* suggested that the balm of Gilead was pistachio resin. I had no particular use for either bit of information, except that I found them interesting.

At three o'clock Anthony made a phone call. *The* phone call. Even from where I was sitting, I could hear the ring tone. After the fifth, I heard her voice. The recording was bare bones. I'm not available right now, please leave your name and number. At least it was her voice. Visibly disappointed, and not a little puzzled, Anthony rang off.

I gave him a moment. "If it helps," I said, "I think I saw her in the Union just after chem lab. She was walking away from me, so I can't be sure. But she looked okay, as far as I could tell."

Anthony gave me a speculative appraisal. "You wouldn't happen to be in any of her classes."

"No, but—" And I stopped there.

"I would not ask you to break a promise," he said. "But I feel that this is a very troubled young lady."

I started. "Not suicidal, you don't think."

"No. I think she described herself accurately. She's lost."

I considered that. "I can tell you this. At one point she told me the classes she was taking. She listed three, but before she could tell me the fourth, she just stopped. She didn't even utter a syllable."

He folded his hands together as if in prayer. "Curious."

"It was almost as if revealing the title of the course would tell me too much about herself."

"That is a fair assessment. Not necessarily accurate," he hedged. "But fair."

"Would you mind a question that is probably personal?"

"Not at all. What is it?"

"After you listen to a client, you close your eyes. Are you praying?"

His smile was that of a saint. "Yes, of course."

"To...whom?"

"Saint Anthony. I've told you this." He flashed a grin and added, "It's cover for my magic."

In retrospect, given what ultimately transpired, I could recall several little remarks like this, as if he were leaving a trail of breadcrumbs that led to the truth.

I told him what I had done with Benj Davis the night before. He nodded approval after I finished.

"What was your state of mind when you uttered this 'mantra,' as you call it?" he asked me.

"Do you mean, did I think it would work?"

"What were you thinking, what...were you believing?"

Not for the first time in this office, I caught a glimmer of light. "I was addressing Saint Anthony," I told him. "I believed he would help me sort this out."

"You had faith in him."

"Faith, yes."

"And after this 'mantra,' this invocation, you found the right questions to ask. Questions that directly resulted in finding the receipt."

More light flashed. "But that's what you do. Isn't it?"

He had the smile of someone who knew something that I did not. "The 'mantra' of which you spoke consisted of simple words," he said. "Your faith is in the reality represented by those words. Words and reality are characteristics of all forms of faith."

I nodded, though I understood little. He gave me a few moments to let his words sink in, but I knew I would be pondering them for a while.

"What should we do about Leah?" I asked.

"She has to come to us. Go on home, Eric. I'll see you tomorrow after class."

003

Although I was not exhausted when I reached the apartment, I flopped down on the bed with Anthony's statement ringing in my ears, haunting me. Well I knew the words applied to me. "She has to come to us." I closed my eyes and drew several long slow breaths, and went back to a time almost four years ago.

At fifteen, my parents had died in a traffic accident. I was to become a ward of the state, that is, an orphan in search of a foster home. Had I thought of it then, I might have spoken with a priest. But my parents, though Catholic, had been rather casual about their religious practices, and that careless attitude had rubbed off on me. Mass was an inconvenience.

I had nowhere to go, so I ran away. I lived on the street. I attended my high school classes, not so much for the learning, although I did well enough, but because the school would have reported me missing or truant, had I not attended. I forged permission papers. I stayed here and there with friends, or with those whom I thought were friends. Money was scarce. I had a few irregular jobs; putting advertising fliers on windshields, mowing lawns, and so on. Stealing supplemented the meager income. Without going into detail, I was a mess outside of school.

I never lost sight of God, however. I paid scant attention to Him, yet spoke now and then with Him as if He were a friend. Still, prayer was somehow beneath me. One day in my senior year I needed groceries, and decided to hit a food pantry at Our Lady of the Light. It was easy enough. The patio where people received groceries was open, as was the storage shack that I had targeted. If you look like you know where you're going and what you're doing, people who are otherwise working pay little attention to you. Carrying a clipboard sometimes helps. I got inside the shack and filled two plastic bags as if I were preparing them for one of the clients in the line outside. On the way off the patio, I tripped and fell headlong onto concrete.

Even as I landed, a man was there to see whether I was all right and to help me to my feet. I had saved the bags, and now I placed them on a table, as if they were donations. But the assistance and concern had only begun. A second man found a folding chair and set it up for me. A third brought me a chilled bottle of water. A fourth kept passing his index finger in front of my eyes; I supposed he was checking for concussion, but I hadn't hit my head. Finally I crossed my eyes at him, and he laughed.

Presently I felt better, and left. Walking slowly; it was a warm and sunny day, and the water in the bottle refreshed me; I passed a park and stopped, to sit down on a bench. Because something was bothering me, and I could not set it aside. I had to work it out.

It took a good part of the afternoon to figure it out, but it came down to this. I was a complete stranger to those four men. Yet they came to my assistance as if I were their brother. I, who was stealing from them, although I doubted that they realized this. In pondering all this, I realized what was missing from my life. After my parents died, I did not belong anywhere. I needed to belong to something, some sort of community, and especially the sort of community where strangers helped one another, even without being asked. I needed to go back to church. Specifically, that church: Our Lady of the Light. Because I had been given a light, and without having asked for it. I needed to belong to something that was bigger than I was.

But how?

Well, in my heart I knew what I had to do. But I was afraid to take the first step. I discovered that I was ashamed of the life I had been leading, especially after my parents died. Resolved I was not to...well, not to sin anymore, but in order to get into the graces of the Church, I had to tell someone. I had to reveal my shame, to acknowledge my guilt. I had to go to Confession.

The Church was not going to come to me; I had to go to the Church. And I couldn't do it. I was afraid. And ashamed. And embarrassed. Yet I could not become a member of the community I sought in good standing without Confession. Oh, I was sorry now for the things I had done. That was not an issue. But I had to tell someone. I had to tell a priest. I had to confess, and repent.

How, how, how?

In the meantime, I talked with God. This was something else that I could not reveal, lest someone think me insane. And in the meantime, I found some more odd jobs. I still lived on the street, and sometimes slept in parks. I came to understand, to know, what I had to do, regardless of the consequences. I had to go to Confession. There simply was no alternative.

The realization, however, was not the act. I put it off. One Saturday it was raining. There was no reason for that to stop me from going to Confession, but I let it stop me. Next week, I told myself. Next Saturday. But next week I had a job offer, and I was hungry. Oh, I could have gone to Confession after I delivered the groceries for the store...but I didn't go. I had an excuse. But finally...

Finally it was time to stop making excuses. I had to go. I had to grit my teeth and erase all worry and fear, and go, just go. All I could say as I walked to the Church was oh, God, oh God, oh God.

I was close to petrified. I was going to admit to shame, to sin.

Worse, I went inside Our Lady of the Light at three in the afternoon, the appointed time when the priest heard Confessions—and found that the priest had not arrived! Another excuse; it bore on me powerfully...but this time I couldn't leave. I had to stay. I had to see this through, fear and shame or no fear and shame.

I sat in the pew by the Confessional office and waited. It was a small measure of relief that no other penitents were present. Nobody to know that I was going to Confession. That I had sins to confess. As a distraction, I took in my surroundings. The church itself in no way resembled a cathedral. It looked as if it had been a warehouse, now remodeled and with stained glass windows. A simple affair, with a nave and an altar, and a stand by the wall for the tabernacle. An apse to the left had been expanded to make a chapel for private ceremonies such as small weddings and baptisms. Above the tabernacle, in stained glass, was the Virgin Mary, dressed in blue and white, the patron of this particular church. To her right as I faced her was a crucifix that I thought was wrong, because it depicted Jesus's spear wound in his right side, and I had always thought it was in his left. Maybe I was looking for any distraction from what I had to do.

The only other place that caught my eye was to the small chapel. I could just see part of it from where I was sitting. Part of an altar, a pot of flowers, a stained-glass window depicting the Marriage at Cana, half of a pew. For private ceremonies and worship, I thought again, and drifted back to thoughts of confessing my sins.

In that moment, it came to me that I did not have to do this, to go to Confession. I had *chosen* to do it. But at the time, I did not know what that meant.

The priest arrived, in black with the white collar. He smiled as he passed me. He was probably sixty, tall and slender, his hair all gray and neatly combed, but he looked ten or fifteen years younger than sixty. He entered the confession room, picked up a stole, kissed it, and put it on.

And beckoned to me.

The room featured in one corner a statue of Jesus being scourged, and in the other half of the room there was a partition behind which the priest sat. On my side of the partition was a place to kneel. But there was also a wooden armchair with a cushioned seat that faced him behind the partition, and I sat down there. I was trying to be brave. To show myself that I was not afraid. I don't think he heard my heart pounding. I made the Sign of the Cross and somehow recalled the ritual words, adapting them to the time I had been away.

"Bless me, Father, for I have sinned. It has been five years since my last confession."

Father Padraig—for that was his name—did not even blink.

I fell into a conversational mode. I explained that it might be easier for me to use the Ten Commandments as a mnemonic device, and go through each one and explain how I had violated it. He said that was okay, that many people sometimes did that to help clear their minds and make a good confession.

It's difficult to be tense and relaxed at the same time. I managed it, because Father Padraig made it easy to talk to. Confession became, not a ritual, but a conversation of sorts. There was nothing to fear, nothing to be afraid of. Just tell the priest what you've done. When I reached the Adultery Commandment, which had to do with sex, I mentioned…well, masturbation. Still he did not blink.

I took a few breaths. I was relaxed now without fear. I was still ashamed, and I still am, for that matter, but it's over, it's done, and I'm free. I made my Act of Contrition, received Absolution, and found that I weighed about four pounds. I was free.

But I was not done. There was Penance. While meditating on the crucifix, I was to say five Hail Marys, one for each of Jesus's wounds. Father Padraig was including the crown of thorns as a wound, while I considered each foot as a wound. Not that it mattered, because…

I attended Mass the next day. I arrived early, so that I could do my Penance. I discovered that the rosary was being told before Mass. So I said my Hail Marys along with them, and wound up saying thirty-five instead of five. I focused on the right hand of Jesus…and that was as far as I got. I never made it to the other four wounds.

Remember, I was supposed to meditate. So I thought about the kind of death that was crucifixion. It was death by suffocation. Hanging from the cross stretches the chest muscles, tightening them, gradually making it difficult and then impossible to breathe. The dying process takes hours, sometimes even a day. It's a horrible and horrific way to die. But I speculated that Jesus did not die of suffocation, because he bled out. He shed every drop of blood. When the spear bit his side, a bit of red-tinted water came out. He shed every drop for…

And that's when a mallet hit me: He died that horrible death because of the things I had done.

Yes, I took it personally. He actually died to remit all the sins that had ever or would ever be committed. But I took it personally. I sent Him to his death because of my sins.

The realization stunned me. It does to this day.

Through it all, I still said all the Hail Marys. But they were meditative chants, not prayers. I was focused on my guilt, and on His death for me. In church, I wept.

The Mass that followed was an old friend. I had gone several times as a child and into my early teens. The liturgical responses came readily enough. Father Padraig gave me Communion. I was home.

But things had changed. I did not know who I was now, or where I was going. I had another mantra whenever I talked with God. "Please keep me on the path today and give me the light to see it by." Only later did I learn that this was similar to a line in Psalm 119.

Who am I and where am I going? Well...I'm going that way. If I misstep, God will put me back on track. As for who I am...

Which is how I met Anthony Lost. As I left Mass, Father Padraig was saying goodbye to his parishioners, and when I came to shake his hand, he told me that Anthony was looking for a reliable assistant.

Ta-dah!

But in recalling all this as I lay on the bed, I realized that Leah and I had something in common: we were both afraid of what we had to do.

I meant to keep that in mind, the next time I saw her. And somehow I knew there would be a next time.

004

Sometimes there is simply nothing to do. I had classes on Wednesday and Friday, and on Thursday put almost an entire eight hours in the Foundry with Anthony. But no one had lost anything, the classes passed as usual and with a lot of reading, and Leah Hawthorne had made no contact. Nor had I seen her on campus, although to be fair I was not looking very hard. You can't force a random encounter; it has to happen by chance. Pardon my tautology.

Which left me to Saturday. The Foundry was closed, although I knew Anthony sometimes spent a few hours in the office. Benj got his rent paid.

Candy Sunquist, who lives in the apartment on the other side of mine, came over for a while, and we played cribbage and kept a Tigers game on low. Like me, she's a sophomore at The City University, but she's majoring in Fine Arts. She has had a steady job for three years at a candy store, thus her nickname. She was born Rebecca. She's tallish and slender, with a mop of short curly black hair. Soaking wet in her clothes, she might clear a hundred pounds. She plays cribbage like the cartoon version of the Tasmanian devil, and won all three games that we played. After the last game ended, I put a DVD on, and we sat on the sofa and watched *Alice in Wonderland*—the Mia Wasikowska version—and threw popcorn at one another. Afterwards we talked about this and that, and just after sunset she went back to her place.

I straightened up the room, and fell asleep on the sofa while reading a magazine. It was just after ten when I got up and went to bed.

Which took me to Sunday.

There's only one Mass at Our Lady of the Light. I usually arrived well before nine, but on this particular day

I made it with just a few minutes to spare. The pew I usually chose was already fairly full, so I genuflected at the pew behind and pulled the missal and hymnal from the slot, using the bulletin I'd gotten at the door as a bookmark for the start of the Mass. The three hymns chosen for this Sunday were posted on a column off to the right. I checked the numbers and found none of the three to be familiar. Two candles lit the altar. This was a green day, and so would Father Padraig's chasuble be.

To the left of the altar, Mary Kline, one of the lectors, began strumming opening chords on her guitar, and the congregation stood for the opening procession. The first hymn began. I watched the three altar servers lead the way up the aisle, the one in front carrying a pole with a cross on top, with Father Padraig bringing up the rear. In the pew behind me, two or three voices were singing more vocally than the others around me. I hadn't realized that pew was occupied. I kept my eyes on the stained glass window in the wall behind the altar, where the Virgin Mary seemed to greet everyone.

Mass is usually the same. The ritual makes it easy to forget that you're part of a ritual, so that you can think about your life and the things you need to work on, and the words—as Anthony put it—that lead to the realities of what we believe. So I said the Kyrie and sang the Gloria and recited the *Credo*, and thought about what they meant. I listened to the Bible passages and the sermon, and found some words relevant to the life I was now leading. Eventually we came to the part where Father Padraig said, "Let us offer each other the sign of peace."

I shook hands with the three men and two women in front of me, and the man just down the pew from me, and turned around to find Leah Hawthorne standing with arm outstretched, and shocked to see me.

Hesitantly she took my hand, and held it for perhaps a beat longer than necessary. She neither smiled nor frowned, but turned her attention to the man next to me, said the usual, "Peace be with you," and I turned back around, with a, "Whoa! Now what?" rumbling through my brain.

But the time had come for Communion. In preparation I whispered a mantra: I'm about to take you inside of me so that I can be inside of you. I waited my pew's turn, stepped into the aisle, and forward in the procession. Whether Leah was directly behind me was now a moot point, as I focused on who I was about to receive. Another mantra entered: *stay with me, God; I'll be worth it.* And that thought remained until I reached the pew again, and dropped to my knees for a meditation.

With Mass officially ended, the congregation filed out of the church, most of them shaking hands or otherwise greeting Father Padraig as he stood at the entrance with one of the servers. After I said hello and walked on, I felt a tug at my arm. Certain who it had to be, I turned back around, only to find an older woman who thrust a folded church bulletin at me.

"You dropped this," she said pleasantly.

I was so shaken by my false expectations that I absently accepted the bulletin and tucked it into my pocket. Meanwhile, I looked around for any sign of Leah Hawthorne, who had been wearing a dull brown blouse tucked into rather loose blue jeans. But she had already vanished.

Back in the apartment, I discovered two folded bulletins in my pocket. Brow tightened, I opened the one that the woman had handed me, and found the hand-scribbled note: it was a phone number, under which had been scrawled, "I'm frightened."

Now I had some ethics to consider. If Leah was anyone's client, she was Anthony's. Helping her find herself was his challenge, not mine. But the Foundry would not be open until tomorrow. Factor in the nondisclosure promise I had made to her. Factor in, too, that Anthony had sent me to the restaurant with her so that she might talk to me. The simple fact was that I probably knew more about her than he did, but he knew a lot more about how to help her. A mistake on my part could well drive her away.

I clawed the air and made a pirate sound (argh!).

Factor in as well that I would not mind seeing Leah again.

I held my breath and tokked the phone number. She picked up before the second ring, as if she had been perched over the phone in expectation or in hope. Or both.

"What I don't understand," I said, before we even greeted one another, "is who that older woman was."

Her blinking was palpable. "Who?" I explained what had happened, and she said, "Apparently I didn't get it far enough into your pocket. Can you come over?"

My brain said, "I don't think that's a good idea." What came out of my mouth was, "Where are you?"

Leah was a short bus ride from me. I had three minutes to catch the Number 11, and made it just as the driver was pulling the bus to the curb. Twelve minutes later I was standing at the secure front door of an old brownstone tenement complex, waiting for her to buzz me in. The building itself dated back toward the beginning of the previous century, but it had been maintained. The window frames of the bottom row of apartments looked relatively new, the white paint on them even newer, and the best indicator of care was the front lawn and the grass on the easement, which was trimmed and neat and free of debris. An old but serviceable assembly of dwellings.

She lived on the second floor. She had the door ajar, a response to the echoes of my footsteps in the hallway. She had been crying, but had dried her eyes, as if she were hoping it would not show. Sympathy was not her goal. She pulled the door and bade me enter.

The apartment was obviously that of someone who lived alone and rarely, if ever, received guests. Not that it was a mess; far from it. The only room immediately visible was the living or front room, appointed by a short sofa sandwiched between end tables; a Queen Anne chair—which I recognized because my mother had one; a coffee table on which was stacked a pile of magazines; a desk that bore a computer stack and a printer/fax; and a five-caster rotating chair in the desk well. Against the wall beside the desk stood a four-shelf bookcase—the kind you can buy from a box store and assemble yourself. It was loaded with books, and more had been laid flat across the top row. Striking by its absence was the utter lack of visual entertainment—no television set, no DVD player, only a small and basic CD player on the sill of the bay window, next to a couple of potted plants.

But the desk was cluttered, the stack of magazines had not been tamped straight, an empty coffee cup stood under a lamp on one of the end tables, and only one of the two curtains that covered the bay front window had been drawn. I did not see any CDs anywhere, but perhaps she kept them in the bedroom. That's where I keep mine.

The kitchen—more properly a dinette—had a gas stove, a refrigerator, and a dishwasher, standard appliances all. A small dining table with four straight-backed wooden chairs marked the boundary between the kitchen and the front room. Speckled white and brown linoleum defended the wood floor underneath. A few dishes sat idly on the counter by the sink. An opened loaf of 12-grain bread awaited attention beside the toaster. The coffeemaker was empty and idle. A short hallway led, presumably, to the bathroom and the solitary bedroom.

The apartment was more refuge than home. Looking it over, I realized I had expected as much.

"Do I pass?" Leah asked, somewhat miffed.

I quickly apologized, and temporized. "In some ways, it looks like my place."

She had changed from her church outfit to a pastel blue jersey, blue jeans cut off just above the knees, and open-toed tan sandals. From a fine silver chain around her neck dangled a silver crucifix. Apparently my arrival had caught her either putting on or removing her earrings, as only the left ear bore one, a simple silver piece with a teardrop gemstone pendant.

Again she asked whether she passed. I averted my eyes. "Sorry." The obligatory question followed. "Are you all right? You said you were frightened."

She did not respond directly. "Would you like something to drink? A soda? Or I could brew some coffee."

"I wouldn't want you to go to any trouble."

"Coffee it is, then," she said, and moved off toward the kitchen. "I have an Italian roast," she said, with a glance over her shoulder at me.

"That's sounds good."

Maybe she was now procrastinating, a defense mechanism. Maybe, now that I was here, she was uncertain with regard to what she wanted. Anthony says you have to let them get at it their own way. Sometimes it takes a deep breath and a burst of courageous will. I should know; that's what got me to Confession.

The coffeemaker soon began to burble. Slowly Leah stepped toward me, a host receiving a guest again. Arms across her chest, hands clasping her elbows, classically defensive, she paused three paces away. Her expression said she had yet to make up her mind about something. I had already broached the topic of her fright, and saw no reason to prod her about it. Either she would or would not tell me.

"Thank you for coming," said Leah.

"The invitation was hard to resist."

"Why am I frightened? Yes, I know. But it's not what you might think...it's like I told Mr. Lost, Anthony. I don't know what I'm supposed to do."

I moved toward the sofa and sat down at one end of it. Leah followed, and sat down carefully at the other end, just out of arm's reach. I said, "Do about what?"

She shook her head. Loose brown hair flowed over one shoulder and then the other. "That's not what I... Eric...I-I meant, mean, I don't know what God wants me to do."

I found a little smile for her. Not one of amusement, but of sympathy. "I assume you pray."

"I didn't realize you attended the same church. No, that's not quite accurate. The truth is that I never even thought about it. When you turned around, you gave me quite a start."

I gave a light laugh. "About like the start I had."

Leah laughed as well. "I can imagine. Eric, to answer your question, yes, I do pray. For guidance, for help...I'm not even sure I know what I'm asking for."

"Please keep me on the path today," I whispered. "And give me the light to see it by."

"That's...that's beautiful," she breathed.

"I talk with God every morning, Leah. That's what I start with."

She thought about that. "Stealing."

"You're welcome to it."

She seemed to relax then. One arm topped the arm rest, the other fell to her lap as she twisted slightly toward me. Abruptly she barked a laugh. "Sausage link, you called me."

"A confused one, as I recall." I turned to face her. "Leah, you said you were studying Humanities. Aside from the fact that it's a required course, is there another reason for taking it?"

"I hoped it might help me with self-discovery," she replied. "But my compass has lost its magnetism, and Polaris is too faint to be seen."

The manner in which she used words suggested another direction. "Do you like poetry?" I asked.

She frowned. "What does that have to do with it? I mean, yes, but what...?"

"You spoke like a poet just then. You used a couple of gentle metaphors."

"Oh." Her brain went into high gear. "Oh, yes, I see." She found a smile that seemed more for herself, as if at some private thought. "How many names do I have to give you in order to prove myself?"

"I like Eliot and Yeats."

She brightened considerably. "Oh, so do I! *Practical Cats.*"

"*The Song of Wandering Aengus?*"

"And that one," she added, still excited. "I have a copy of Ray Bradbury's *The Golden Apples of the Sun*, and looked up where he got that title from. When I read the poem..." Her face fell flat and sad, and she looked away.

"Leah?" I worried.

She spoke as if from the farthest star, in a voice as fragile as an old wine. "It's the glimmering girl Yeats was searching for. But I don't know whether I am the girl or the searcher. It's like, I don't know, hiraeth, maybe, or *Tír na nÓg*, someplace you can dream of reaching, but you can never quite reach it. Shangri-La, or maybe Xanadu. You know they exist, but..." And tears gathered in her blue eyes and began to trickle down her cheeks.

Had I known her better, I might have reached out for her, to comfort her. But a hug of comfort, however well-meaning, was risky. She had revealed something of her soul to me, and I recognized it because I had been there myself. I was, in fact, still there.

"Leah?"

She turned completely to face me and drew her legs up onto the sofa, tucking them under her. She was not ashamed of her tears, although she thumbed them away. "Are you going to tell me that maybe I'm looking for God?" she blurted.

"Are you?"

She shook her head. "I know where God is," she said. "I just haven't found..."

"What did you expect to find?"

She braved a smile. "That's a question out of the Bible."

"Which you've read, it seems."

"Mostly the New Testament. Some of the Old. It's not talked about much in the Humanities class."

"Not these days, it wouldn't be. Leah—"

She raised a hand, stopping me. "Don't. I know what you're going to say. God is easy to find if you look for Him. He's with you wherever you go. Just talk to Him. But I-I-I...oh, I don't know what to say."

"Just say hello."

She blinked. "Is it that easy? Oh, it can't be that easy."

"It is for me."

"For you. Oh, I don't even know you."

"And yet you're baring your soul to me. But Leah, I'm not the one who you should be talking to. I'm just the assistant. Anthony is the one with the words and the experience. You can tell him everything you've told me."

She shook her head. "You're easier to talk to. You listen too much."

"It's hard to hear with your mouth open."

She dismissed this. "I guess."

"Leah, God listens a lot better than I do."

"But...but what do I say?

The question was a breakthrough of sorts. "You can pray, of course. But you can also sit here, as you are with me, and talk about Keats and Yeats and Eliot, or a magazine article, or maybe you tried to make biscuits and they came out as hockey pucks. Leah, God isn't someone you need to summon, like me. He isn't on some distant cloud, waiting for you to dial His phone. God is always here, right here, because He is everywhere. God always knows everything, including about those biscuits and those poets. But you're holding back. You haven't...I don't know, meshed with Him. Tell Him what you think, how you feel. Sure, He knows these things, but by telling Him, you've brought yourself into a relationship with Him. It starts with, 'Hello, God, good morning.'

"Did you ever say, or hear, that bedtime prayer of 'Now I lay me down to sleep?" Leah nodded hesitantly. "When you finish it, go over your plans for the next day. Things you need to do. Say them out loud, because you're talking with God. Sometimes, what happens to me is, when I go through those next-day plans, I'll realize I've forgotten to mention something. That, Leah, is God whispering in my ear. Like, oh, yeah, I gotta remember to send a birthday card to someone, or there's a book I wanted to start reading. Things like that. General stuff. Like we say to one another. Leah, God is your friend. Treat Him like one. Worship, yes, adore, yes, pray, yes, but be friends, too."

Leah's breathing had grown ragged and shallow. It might have been the effect of what I had told her, or perhaps she had found in the words a glimmer of light, illuminating a path she had not known was there. Even both. Her eyes were half-closed now. I kept silent. Whatever this was, it was for her to reason out.

I don't know what she might have said, but she looked away, and suddenly her eyes went wide. "It's almost noon," she cried. "I'm supposed to meet Mom." She gained her feet in a fluid motion. "I'm sorry, but...we're going shopping, and then to dinner."

The inevitable was difficult to accept at that moment. She had been thinking about what I had said. But where would she have gone with it?

"It's all right," I assured her. Already she was rushing about. Perhaps she was listening. "Leah, tomorrow go see Anthony and tell him everything you've told me. I have morning classes, but I'll be there in the afternoon."

She nodded. I showed myself out, and caught the bus back to my apartment. A bit of emptiness had set in; I had missed an opportunity. But an opportunity for what?

I lost myself in a pizza and the textbooks for tomorrow's two classes.

005

Monday afternoon was even more empty, for Leah did not show up at the Foundry, nor did she call. Anthony did almost have a client. The man was slightly paunchy and not a little florid. Light gleamed off a head fringed with graying black hair. His facial color was not reflective of his mood; he was amiable enough. He spoke a little louder than necessary in the small office, a man who was accustomed to being the center of attention. He introduced himself as Robert Maxwell, call me Buddy. Despite his tone, about him was a touch of diffidence, of hesitation, as if he were not certain that he was in the right place.

Maxwell arrived five minutes after I did. Today I had brought a folding metal chair, so I had somewhere to sit while Maxwell took up the client's chair. I gave him my best reassuring smile when he glanced over his shoulder at me.

Finally he got to it. "I understand you find things that are lost."

Anthony folded his hands on top of the desk and leaned a little closer, though certainly not to hear better. "That is a simple way of putting it," he agreed. "What did you lose?"

He looked from side to side, slightly embarrassed. "Forty-one thousand dollars."

Unlike myself, Anthony did not bat an eyelash. "In an envelope?" he asked. "Or some other container?"

"Well...no."

Anthony waited.

"It's...I lost it in Reno."

"I...see. What were the circumstances?"

"Well...I was at the...first I was at the Blackjack table, then at the, the Roulette wheel. So I thought...so I had heard about you, and I thought maybe...you could help me."

Anthony sadly shook his head. "But your money is not lost," he pointed out. "You know exactly where it is."

"Well...yes, I suppose so. But I *lost* it!"

"I understand, Mr. Maxwell," he said placidly. "But it is not the sort of lost item that I locate. It's a different kind of 'lost,' you see."

Maxwell's sigh came loud and long. His voice had lost some of its boom. "I...well, I thought...thought I would try." He got up.

"I'm sorry I can't help you, Mr. Maxwell. I could give you some advice, but I'm sure you know what it would be."

"Yeah, I guess I do." He made a little wave. "Thank you, anyway."

After the door closed behind Maxwell, I pressed my lips together. "Give it a couple minutes," said Anthony, choking back his own laughter. "Let him get out of hearing range."

"I feel sorry for him."

"As do I. But my advice is the fix, and I doubt he would follow it." He sat back. "When you came in, you looked like you had something to tell me."

I moved to the stuffed chair. "I saw Leah Hawthorne yesterday. She attended Mass, and by chance was in the pew directly behind mine. When I turned for the sign of peace..."

"Surprise."

I laughed. "As we filed out of the church, she stuck a note into my pocket." I gave him the details of that. "If it hadn't been for that woman..."

"You have no idea who she is? You've never met her?"

I shook my head. "She's a parishioner, that's all. I may have seen her at some point, but not memorably."

Anthony steepled his fingers on top of the desk. "Interesting. Curious."

"Fortuitous."

"That as well," he agreed. "What did the note say?" I told him, and he thought about it for a moment or two. "I think it is possible," he said slowly, with a bit of hush in his tone, "that woman's rescue of the note was an intervention from God. We don't often see events in this way, but happenstance is not always happenstance, Eric. You called Leah, of course. It was meant that you call her."

"She invited me over to her apartment," I told him, and hesitated. "That's where I have a problem. Remember, I promised her. And I'm not sure that what we said to one another doesn't fall under that promise." I sighed. "In any case, it might be a moot point, as I recommended strongly that she—"

The front door opened. My heart lurched as I turned back. But it was the letter carrier who walked in. She greeted Anthony by name, laid a couple envelopes on the desk, and departed with a nod of hello for me.

Anthony did not so much as glance at the envelopes. "You were expecting her."

I acknowledged as much. "But if she doesn't show…"

"Then you have to keep your promise, Eric. But is there anything you can tell me, keeping it general?"

Dragging fingers through my hair and rubbing my head failed to make things clearer. "She reads Yeats and Eliot, among others," I told him. Trying to pick and choose what I felt I could tell him was like poking my way through a bramble. "She does not realize that you can talk with God, not only in prayer, but in the way you and I are talking now. And she mentioned *Tír na nÓg* in context."

"The Irish far-off place?"

He seemed to know what that implied, and I left it there. Worried now about Leah, I checked the clock: just after two-thirty. Please show, please show. "There's nothing to be afraid of," I whispered.

Anthony gave me a tilt of his head, an unspoken question. Then he glanced past my shoulder. "I think you had better switch chairs," he said.

I got up and turned around to watch Leah open the door.

Unbidden, I poured a mug of coffee for her, fixing it the way she liked it. I asked her whether she wanted me to leave, and she shook her head. She had been crying not long ago. She was neatly dressed in casual clothes—jersey and jeans, both blue, which made it impossible for me not to think of her eyes. She was sitting with her arms on the armrests, and with legs crossed at the knees. The fingers of her left hand slipped through the loop of the mug, clutching it firmly. She was in control of herself.

Blessed with a phonographic memory, she was able to relate our conversations at *Waffle World* and in her apartment almost word-for-word. She spoke evenly, for the most part, with a few words that passed in a constricted voice, as if she were on the verge of tears but winning the battle. The overall tension in her tone was palpable, and I knew her visit had taken the same sort of courage that had gotten me into the confessional. With a few words and phrases added to clear up any murkiness, the process took us to a quarter till four. Through it all, Anthony asked no questions, but he had several after she had finished.

"Sausage links?" he asked, and she and I broke into laughter—Anthony's way of relieving some tension.

"Leah, have you had any religious instruction?" he asked.

"I attended St. Rita's for six years," she replied. "I had to memorize the catechism. But rote memory is not understanding."

"True enough," he agreed. "The words have to be applied to actions, but if you don't know the actions, the words are nice enough, but without apparent application. Have your parents added to your religious upbringing?"

She answered carefully. "They are...casual church-goers. I'm trying...I'm *trying*, to be regular at that, I-I...it's very possible that the answers I seek will be found...in association with the church. But I don't know what I'm looking for."

"You've been Baptized? Confirmed?" She nodded. "Are you open to suggestion?"

She looked confused, and shifted position in the chair. "I-I don't understand."

"You spoke at length about what Eric said about talking with God as a friend," Anthony explained. "God, and particularly the Holy Spirit, has been known to implant nudges into your mind. A thought you hadn't considered, or a reminder of something, or even a seemingly-unrelated word or two that, when pondered, seems to take you in a new direction."

"I-I haven't had such a, a nudge."

"Of course you have. You came here last week. You're here again. You expect to find something, but you don't know what it is." He sat back. "Yet."

"Wait. You think I'm here because God nudged me?"

"I think it's possible, yes."

Leah glanced at me. "But it was Eric who urged me to come today."

"But he did not even know to make contact with you until a complete stranger kindly picked up your note that had fallen from his pocket and returned it to him."

"And you're saying...saying God...God what? Made certain the woman was in the right place and at the right time, and in a helpful mood?"

"It is certainly possible, Leah. Without that note, you would not have spoken with Eric, nor would you be here now."

Leah fell silent. I started to speak, but Anthony raised a hand to stop me. The message was clear: she's thinking about something. A minute and more passed, pregnant with possibilities.

"So certain random events that might otherwise be inexplicable could be attributed to divine intervention," she said at last. "Either explanation is reasonable, so it comes down to what you believe."

Anthony nodded emphatically. "I could not have said it better myself."

Leah sighed. "That brings us to faith," she said. "And I don't know what faith is."

"Faith is a gift from God," Anthony told her. "Just ask for it. You'll find it at the right time." He leaned forward, fingers steepled. "Now, Leah, as to your search for self. I'm going to help you find you in what is for me an unconventional way. Oh, I'll be here for consultation, questions, recommendations, and advice. But I'm going to let Eric here work with you."

"What?" Leah and I said together. I added, "I can't. I mean, I don't know how..."

"You've had an effect on Leah," Anthony pointed out. "Just be yourself. I think it's working for her."

Words fled me. I had no idea what to say. During my talk with Leah in her apartment, I was just being... well, friendly. She's easy to talk with, once the conversation gets going. Sausage links, indeed.

Leah and I exchanged glances. Her expression was unreadable; mine made the skin of my face tighten. I felt lost again, like I had before my Confession. Probably like Leah was feeling, not from my assignment to her, but in general, in her life. Two lost people. Such a cliché. I could only hope that Anthony knew what he was doing.

But Leah's eyes and face grew sad as she looked at me, as if she were reading my inner conflict. Yesterday, as I called her, I wondered whether this was a good idea. My desire to see her overrode that objection. Sometimes it is difficult to know which voice to listen to.

"May I call you this evening?" I asked her, as she got up to leave.

"I wish you would," she replied, and walked out the door.

My full attention was now on Anthony. Words now flailed me, and it was difficult to assemble them coherently. Finally I managed a, "What are you thinking? This isn't my job. It's not what I hired on for. I'm just a clerk, Anthony. I'm not qualified to—"

"And what, exactly, are the qualifications here?" he broke in. Evidently I'd reached a part in the protest that interested him.

"What? I-I...you mean, *your* qualifications?" I had never thought about that. Anthony just did what he did.

He nodded. "Think about them. Give them some consideration. What, exactly, do I do here?"

"You...you help people find things. Just like Saint Anthony," I added.

"And how do I do that?"

"By...well, by praying, and probably by reasoning things out...I don't know."

"But you're missing the larger picture, Eric."

I had to laugh. "Prayer is not large enough? Receiving a form of divine intervention is not large enough?"

He shook his head in mild disapproval, and he was right, I was missing something. But what?

"What's the first step here?" he asked. "Which aspect of finding takes the longest? What do I do when a client walks in. After introductions, I mean. Eric?"

"Well, you lis— Oh."

"*Précisement, mon ami.* I listen." He now wore a benevolent smile. "It's so obvious to you that you overlooked it. Because that is what you do, Eric. I suspect you have a natural gift for it. A gift, I think, from the Holy Spirit. You find the right things to say. From sausage links, to having a conversation with God.

"Eric, you were sitting behind her, so you were unable to see her face. When she reached the part about the suggestion of a conversation with God, her eyes lit up. It was a wonderful idea, she was thinking. But how to go about it? And you did that, because you said the right things—they came directly from your heart and your mind —*and* because you *listened.*"

"Jesus, Mary, and Joseph." I gaped at him. "You're serious."

His smile widened. "Eric, finding oneself is not like finding a tuning fork behind the piano. It is a project. It will not happen overnight. It didn't with you, right? How long did you search, without even knowing that you were searching?"

That implied something I had not known before. "You...you spoke with Father Padraig about me?" I shook my head. "No, he wouldn't have told you about my confession, but..."

"He *couldn't* have told me, Eric," Anthony said gently. "The confessional is inviolate. And I'm not going to reveal what he did say. I came away from our conversation with the impression that, at this point in your life, this right here is the right place for you. It's not for the pay, it's for the experience."

"And the training," I said.

"Now you're getting it."

"But...but how can you afford me? I mean, it's a standard rate of twenty-five dollars, times what? Ten clients a week, if that many? That wouldn't even cover the rent here."

"It doesn't." Anthony stood up and came round the desk, and perched on a corner of it. "I'm surprised you hadn't mentioned this before. The math is obvious. So I'll tell you, but it's not for public consumption. Father Padraig knows, and so does Bishop Furrier. No one else... but you. I have a stipend from the Catholic Church. It is enough for the rent and utilities, for my room and board, and for incidentals. I can obtain *ad hoc* funds if necessary for a client."

"Because of what you can do?"

"I've always had a...an ability," he explained. "Eventually I learned, thanks to the bishop, who at the time was Monsignor Furrier, that this was a gift from God. You may think of it as channeling Saint Anthony, if you wish. I will say that I do not always receive...guidance regarding a location. Sometimes I am expected to reason it out on my own."

"But one way or another, you're always successful," I said. "At least, as long as I've been here."

"God grants all things. But occasionally He takes His time with the answer." He drew a knee up and clasped his hands around it. "Now I will let you in on a little secret. Leah is not lost. She simply does not know where she is. That's not the same thing. She knows where she wants to go—else why search? But she doesn't know how to get there. She knows there is something or someone to have faith in—that's what she is seeking when she attends Mass. But she doesn't fully realize what—or *who*—is the object of that faith. Oh, she knows it's God: the Father, the Son, and the Holy Spirit. But she has yet to connect God with faith."

I mulled this over, and Anthony was cognizant enough not to interrupt whatever I was thinking. I was not sure what that was, myself. In the end, I still had an assignment.

"So you want me to...?"

He did not respond.

"Do I get any guidance?"

"I will always guide you, whenever you ask it of me. So will God."

A sigh puffed my lips out. I nodded, mostly to myself.

Anthony stood up. "I believe you have a phone call to make."

006

Chinese take-out on the way back to the apartment constituted dinner. After the last of the fried rice was gone, I raised Leah. She seemed a little peeved that I had not called right away.

"I've been sitting here waiting for you," she said, her tone harsh. But she softened. "I suppose you had a briefing from Anthony."

"He had some advice, which I'll keep to myself. Leah, this evening, dinner came first."

"Is that because you did not want to appear too anxious to call me?"

The book of my life was so open that I had not realized, until she said it, that such was the case. "I think I'm supposed to come up with a plan," I told her. "Which will be next to impossible."

"Pray to St. Jude."

"You know your saints. No, what I meant by that was the difficulty in not knowing the expected outcome. What are you hoping to—"

"Eric," she said, and I fell silent. "I don't think phone calls are going to help me much. I prefer face time. I'm not talking Zoom or some other program. I mean you and I maybe at an outdoor patio in front of a coffee shop. Something like that. I'm not really a phone person. I am not compulsively connected to the Universe."

At that, I had to laugh. "We certainly agree on that." I dug out a pad and pen from the desk. "What's your weekly class schedule?" I jotted and studied what she gave me in relation to my own schedule. "It looks like Tuesday and Thursday afternoons are best for us," I decided. "So tomorrow…?"

"So…so soon?"

"Is there a problem?"

For a moment she was silent. Then: "No, no problem. Where do we meet?"

I managed to arrange the geography. "*Meg's* is close to you. Two blocks or so. Three o'clock?"

We agreed, and I rang off, belatedly remembering that I had not asked about her work schedule, or even whether she was employed. I texted Anthony to let him know I would not be in the office tomorrow. There remained for me nothing to do for the rest of the evening except crack open a textbook or two. I muttered to myself in anticipation.

Chemistry lab was endurable, about the best that could be said for it. I need not enumerate the distractions. From class I went directly to the Foundry, for no better reason than that I wanted to gather myself, even though I had said I wouldn't be in. Anthony seemed to understand this, and let me sit quietly, moving to the folding chair only when a client arrived.

He was an older man, probably in his sixties, befuddled as clients sometimes are. Neatly dressed in slacks and white shirt, the collar cinched with a plain blue necktie, and dark brown dress shoes. Graying brown hair long enough to reach the collar, neatly brushed and combed. I resisted the temptation to inspect his manicure. He spoke hesitantly, but in a calm voice.

"I cannot locate my car," he told Anthony, after introductions. "I parked it at the mall nearby here, went inside to place a special order for a pair of shoes for my wife, and when I came out, I was lost. It's a big parking lot."

Anthony smiled. "It's practically a county all its own."

"I have a new, silver-gray Toyota," he went on. "the windows are tinted, so it is difficult to see inside. There are at least a dozen cars like it in the lot, and I didn't want to arouse suspicion by peering into each one. I tried the license plates, but I have a temporary, and so did at least six other vehicles. But there must be some way of distinguishing mine."

Apparently he was too shaken by the experience of loss to look for little telltale signs of ownership. There's always something: a scratch, a bit of road dust, the brand of tires, something. Anthony started to speak, but I had an idea.

"Take out your key fob, Mr. Whiting," I told him, and he did so. "See that red button at the wide end? When you go back to the mall parking lot, press that red button as you walk around. You'll find your car."

You could see the light strike his eyes as he realized he should have thought of that. He fished into his pocket and drew out a wallet. "How much do I owe you?" he asked Anthony.

"No charge," he replied genially.

Whiting gave me a nod of gratitude as he passed by me on the way to the door. After he left, Anthony asked, "Just where did that solution come from?"

"Some people his age are not...well, they're not tech-oriented," I replied. "Their experience is with less complex technology. I just thought..."

"You thought well. It matched my own thought."

"If it hadn't, St. Anthony would have told you."

He mulled that over. "You're seeing Leah this afternoon."

Inwardly I cringed. "You make it sound like it's a date."

"I did not mean to imply that, Eric. Yet...you seem sensitive to the idea."

"I didn't realize it showed. Anyway, we're meeting at a coffee shop. She told me she prefers face time."

"I think that's wise," he said. "Conversation is not just about voice and tones and hesitations. On the phone, unless you have visual, you cannot see expressions change, or the ways the eyes regard you, or hand and body gestures. It's all words."

"I'll keep that in mind in Sociology tomorrow."

"What do you think you might talk with Leah about?"

I shook my head. At the moment, I had no idea. "I think I should just get to know her first," I said. "And she me."

"It's supposed to rain this afternoon," he reminded me.

"It's a patio table. It has an umbrella. Big red and white one, like a circus."

"And when she walks home?"

"By then it will have stopped raining. Anyway, we can always talk about the weather. That's a conversation starter."

"Universally. All right, off you go. And Eric? Avoid rushing it or pressing. This will unfold as it will."

"Sociology 101," I said, and left for the bus stop.

I did not know whether Leah realized it, but I had chosen *Meg's* mostly because it was close to her apartment. Now I had to wonder about my own motives. Had I chosen the shop for her convenience, or because the conversation might evolve to an invitation to her place? I made a mental note, inscribed on stone, that I was here on assignment. Weak, but it would have to do.

Anthony had been right: rain was in the forecast. Darker clouds had already begun to dim the sunlight. Still, the air itself was calm, in motion with but the faintest of warm breezes. I got off the bus half a block from *Meg's* and hurried toward the clutch of round white patio tables under their umbrellas. Already Leah had arrived, and her face creased into a happy smile when she spotted me. She had already ordered coffee and cinnamon rolls, along with a bowl of glazed donut holes. I sat down across from her, and for a long moment we simply regarded one another.

I found myself wondering what she was thinking. My own thoughts were roiled. She was lovely, easy on the eyes, but she was a client. I had too many conflicts. I found the strength to break eye contact, and to address my roll.

"I'll catch the check," I told her, between bites.

"You're too late," she replied.

"I think it's going to rain."

"I like rain. As long as it's not a cloudburst," she added.

Cautiously I reached across the table to the corner of her mouth. "Bit of frosting," I explained as I fingertipped it away.

"How long have you been working for Anthony?" Leah asked.

"About a year. Next you'll want to know why I'm working for him, and that's a bit of a story."

"I'm listening."

I told her of my dissolute life after my parents died, and how I found myself eventually going to Confession and returning to the Church. I wasn't sure that "returning" was the right word, because even as a child my attendance was irregular.

"My parents gradually fell away," she told me. "I think they're Unitarians now. They're searching for something."

"Just like you."

"Well, not exactly," she said. "I'm where I want to be, church-wise. I believe in God. I believe in the Trinity, although I don't understand it much. But I don't know who I am in relation to God." She peered at me across the table. "Does that make sense?"

I gave a light laugh. "I know that feeling. It can be difficult to relate to someone who is a mystery, whom you can but poorly define."

"So how do you do it?"

"I'm not sure I do. I accept the fact that I believe, that I have faith. For me, it comes down to the fact that God exists. From that, all else follows. Do you know who God is?"

She flashed a shy smile. "I'm still working on that."

"In the Old Testament, God revealed His name to Moses. It's both a name and, if you like, a definition. God said to him, 'I am Who am.' It's the perfect name and definition. 'Who am' means 'always was, is now, and ever shall be.' Just like the Glory Be prayer."

She made a face. "I guess I never thought of it quite that way."

A pensive silence followed. Gradually I realized that we were both eyeing the last donut hole. "Go ahead," I told her.

"No, you take it."

"I don't need the carbs."

She was aghast. "And I do? You want me to be fat?"

"What? No! I mean..."

I settled it in the only way possible: I bit off half of it, and thrust the other half toward her mouth. She accepted this, and lightly licked my fingertip as I withdrew it. Another silence followed as we regarded one another. I had no idea what either of us was thinking, only that I needed a distraction from whatever it was.

"Are you employed?" I asked her.

The abrupt question put her off momentarily. "You mean, how do I pay my rent and tuition. I-I...you're right, the topic is proper between us, given what you are trying to do. I'll return the favor, of course." She sighed. "Eric, my parents pay my tuition and books, and help with the rent. I also work two hours a day at the Union cafeteria, from six to eight in the morning. Overtime on weekends, if I want it, and sometimes I do. I'm not...hurting. I wouldn't mind a different job, but it's hard to find one that would conform to my class hours." She drained her coffee and refilled it from the pot. "Your turn."

I did not tell her that my tuition was paid and that I had no idea who had paid it, although when I queried Anthony, he did not answer. "There's the pay from the Foundry," I said, and hesitated, speaking only after she glared at me. "I, uh, write stories for, for the small independent presses. Science fiction, mostly, and some fantasy. It's not a living, and in no way am I famous, but I've won a couple of small awards, and it's nice to see something I wrote in print."

"I don't believe it. Seriously? You mean I'm sitting here with an actual author?"

I shrugged. "It's really not that big a deal."

"It is to me. Stories, you said. Short stories or novels?"

"I have two novels out. About twenty short stories so far. Leah—"

"I want to read one."

"Only if you tell me the secret subject in your class schedule."

She shook her head. "No, not...not yet. Please don't ask."

"All right."

"Don't be upset. Not with me. Please?"

"I'm not, Leah. I promise."

It started to rain. Only a drizzle, and the umbrella shielded us. The rain grew no stronger, but a little gust of wind showered us briefly.

"So you're what?" she asked. "A storyteller?"

"That's a good word." I shifted gears. "What about you? Do you keep a diary, or a journal?"

"I used to. Why?"

Her tone held a touch of defensiveness. For all our amity, she was still sensitive to personal questions. I made a mental note to tread more carefully.

"Sometimes, writing out your thoughts about who you are and what you're doing can help clarify matters," I said. "Especially if several days later you read what you've written. Sometimes it helps your thought processes."

"Do you keep a diary?"

"I call it a journal, but yes." I flashed a grin. "And before you ask, yes, you are in it."

"As a project, I suppose," Leah said dully.

"Leah, I'm just trying to help. Please believe that. To do that, I need to know more about you."

Her lips tightened, almost bloodless. "I understand, but...I would have thought you'd get to the point."

"There may not be a point. But: all right, then. In what ways don't you know who you are?"

She looked away. "That sounds bad, doesn't it?" It was more statement than question. Her shoulders rose and fell under the pink jersey as she drew a steadying breath. A gust of wind left dark damp spots on the fabric.

"I've been there, Leah," I said quietly. "In some ways, I suppose I'm still there."

She turned back to me. "What happened?"

"After I returned to the Church, I began to consider my relationship to God, to the community of the parish, and even to myself. Who am I, and what am I supposed to do?"

Leah nodded emphatically. "Oh, yeah, I know that one."

I finished the last of the coffee. "We are each capable people, Leah. Everyone on the planet does something. Writing, mining, teaching, sports, something. The list is enormous. Most of us are capable of doing more than one thing. I write stories, and help Anthony help people find things. I experiment with cooking on occasion, and no, don't ask."

Leah laughed.

"So part of who we are, part of our identity, rests in the things we do," I went on. "I can tell by the look in your eyes that you grasp this. Now, religion recently has played a role in both our lives, yours and mine. So maybe the question is, who am I in relation to God? That's one reason why we attend Mass. We're hoping to find some sort of answer there. We'd like to find at least a clue."

Her, "Yes," was almost inaudible.

The drizzle picked up, and I knew this particular discussion had to come to an end. Now I hated the weather; we had just opened a door to something. The words for it had yet to come, but if we kept talking, we might learn something useful in the search for identity. The server came quickly to clear the table. Leah and I stood up, staying under the umbrella as much as possible. For a long moment we looked at one another. I did not know what she or I were thinking.

"I'd better go," she said, breaking that bond.

I could but nod, and watched her run away.

By the time I reached my apartment, I was soaked. I had just gotten into dry clothes when Candy Sunquist showed up at the front door. A bit moist herself, she was porting three containers of Chinese take-out, the invitation implicit. Never one to turn down a free meal, I widened the doorway for her. She went directly to the kitchen table, drew two plates from the cupboard, and began setting up.

"Hungry?" I asked.

"Famished. I missed breakfast. I had to go in to work early." The clatter of plates and forks punctuated her words.

"Well, thanks for this."

"I don't care to eat alone."

"I thought you had a boyfriend," I hinted.

"Rob…" She sighed; her lips tightened as if in pain. "He didn't say it in so many words, but I got the impression he thought he was trading up."

"I'm sorry, Candy."

She sat down, and pointed me to my plate. "I put almost a year into that relationship," she snapped, beginning to seethe at the thought.

"Take a deep breath, Candy."

She did so, and visibly she calmed. "Yeah, yeah. Sorry. I got moo goo gai pan and chicken fried rice, and curry rice."

"You chose well."

She forked a mouthful. "Yeah, I did, didn't I?" But the statement dripped with sarcasm, and I knew she was not referring to the food.

Dimming the overhead light added a bit of intimacy to the meal, and seemed to soothe Candy. Gradually her face grew more serene, and the lighting left parts of her face in shadows. I tried the curry rice.

"Whoo! That's a hot curry."

She got up and went to the refrigerator, and returned with two sodas. "They say lager kills curry, but you don't have any."

"I've another couple months to go," I reminded her, and took several cooling sips, noting that the curry didn't seem to faze Candy. Well, she had ordered for herself. Her visit was the result of having bought too much food.

"Thought you were older."

I had to remind myself that she was twenty-two. "Age is just a number," I said.

"Until you're carded."

Life hit the pause button for a moment.

"Better?" I asked her.

"I don't know. Maybe."

"Would you like to watch a movie?"

She considered that, and said, "I think I want to go back to my place and have a good cry."

"The soda is comfortable," I told her. "You can do that here."

A puzzled frown deepened the shadows on her face. "You said 'soda,' Eric."

"I did not!"

"Did."

"Didn't."

"Did."

"Rabbit season!"

"Duck season!"

We both fell to laughing riotously, even to kicking our legs. I knew then that she was going to be all right. I think she knew that I had deliberately misspoken, but she never said anything specifically about it.

"I do have the *Bugs Bunny Roadrunner* DVD," I said.

"I'll do the popcorn while you set it up. Another sofa?"

I laughed. "Please."

The movie ended, with us hoarse from laughing, even though we'd seen it several times. Candy helped me clean up. She left me the remaining curry rice, and took the rest back to her apartment. When she left, she was a thousand pounds lighter.

007

Wednesday morning in Medieval History and Cultural Anthropology was a drag, for no reason that I could discern. The material, though interesting, was simply blah. The former class covered castles: revetments, battlements, and baileys. The latter consisted of a film of the Trobriand Islanders. I may have dozed off, though I could not be sure.

After the latter class, I stopped by the Student Union on the off-chance that I might encounter Leah Hawthorne, but no such luck. The Foundry was quiet when I arrived, and Anthony had one of those whatsamatta expressions on his face. I shook my head and sat down in the client's chair. The silence between us was deafening and annoying.

Finally I blurted, "I don't think I'm getting through to Leah." I spread the fingers of both hands and held them out in front, and moved them together as if to mesh them. But one hand passed over the other without contact. "Like that," I said. "Have you found anything today?"

"A man came in and asked me whether I knew of any studies of how far a pill will roll once it hits the floor," he said. "In the end, I advised him to work with his pills further onto the desk, so he can catch them before they roll off the edge."

"No charge?"

"He gave me five dollars anyway. I'll put it into the collection on Sunday." He paused. "Eric, is this project getting to you?"

"Leah called it that as well," I told him. "A project. She does not think of herself or her search as a project, and resented the implication. Anthony, I don't want to lose this one. I don't want to lose her."

"Losing this one and losing her are not the same thing, Eric," he said gently. "Are you...becoming involved a little here?"

"No," I said, the opposite of what I meant. I hedged, conceding the point. "Maybe a little. I've had the same questions she has. In some ways, I still have the same questions. I may never obtain the answers. The difference between Leah and me is that I don't let the lack of answers get in the way of my daily life."

He steepled his fingers. "That's an interesting observation. Run with it."

I made an exasperated sound. "There's nothing to run with. We simply have different approaches to our days. Mine works for me, but then if I have questions, I can turn to you or Father Padraig. Leah has no—"

"No one to turn to," he finished for me. "Eric, that's where you have to come into the picture."

"Getting her to talk sometimes is like pulling teeth."

"Someday, someone will come up with a better simile. Eric, a good part of the resolution lies in the discussion, the conversation. Be more alert for openings, and enter them delicately. You've proven to her that she can talk to you. A subtle nudge in a good direction might work wonders. That's how the Holy Spirit inspires us—a little touch here, a quiet word there, and pretty soon we're back on the path and seeing it a little more clearly."

"And I'm not all that knowledgeable in theology," I argued.

"The truth is that much of the intricate workings of what is known about God are best left to the province of the Church," he countered. "She will tell us what we need to know. Most Catholics adhere to the basics: we believe in God, we believe God, we love and adore and worship God, we hark unto the words of God and to the words of the Word and to the breath of the Holy Spirit. Those basics generally lead us to Heaven. If God is in your heart, Eric— and I know that He is—then He will accompany you on this journey, this 'project,' to bring Leah along. Be yourself, Eric. And trust in God."

I sighed, but happily. "Brave words," I said. "Sometimes difficult in execution."

"It's not always easy," Anthony agreed. "But God knows you. He does not expect you to be able to do something you cannot do, physically or mentally. But He does test you; or rather, He puts you in a position where you have to test yourself. Tell me, do you believe that He has brought you to this point where you are in a position to, and have the ability to, help Leah find herself?"

That was a no-brainer. "Yes, of course."

Anthony sat back, satisfied. I sat back, silent with thoughts that were encouraging but not clear. But I knew now that clarification would come along in due time, like a bus to the bus stop—another terrible simile, but such was my thought.

Dinner was leftover curry rice and a garden salad, followed later by a snack of kippered herring. It was time to try some more culinary experiments. I settled on manicotti for the next day. Spinach, onion, and cheese stuffing, a decent spaghetti sauce, and grated parmesan were already making me hungry in anticipation. They also took my mind off Leah.

Benj Davis next door came home from work late. I heard him trudge through the living room, close the refrigerator door a little too solidly, and knock the armchair against the wall as he flopped down. After a brief argument with myself, I went to knock on his door. Instead of opening it, he told me to come in.

Slouched in the armchair, Benj looked despondent. Even his shirt and jeans looked dejected. I parked on the arm of another chair. "Bad day?" I asked him.

For a moment he looked at me as if wondering who I was. Belatedly recognition set in. With a visible effort he sat up a little straighter. "I'm down to twenty hours a week," he muttered. "Almost everyone but the manager and assistants are. And Barkley, the tech whiz, of course."

I nodded grimly. "How bad is it?"

A feeble smile played with the corners of his mouth. "I *like* ramen. Anyway, I'll have to find another job." He gazed up at me with weary brown eyes. "Isn't that what you do? You find things?"

"Only when they're lost. But I'll keep my ears open. Benj, are you going to make your rent?"

He nodded. "Good thing I like ramen."

"If you need a few bucks, I can—"

"No. I don't know that I can pay you back."

"I don't recall asking you to pay it back."

"I-I...all right, okay, if I need help, I'll ask."

"Fair enough," I told him. "Just don't be afraid to ask. Hey, you could come over. I could put a movie on. I have sandwich fixings."

He brightened. "Pastrami? Rye? With a good mustard?"

"So well you know me."

We did not talk much, even during the movie, which was *El Dorado*. Robert Mitchum played the sheriff who recovered from drinking his sorrows away, John Wayne as usual played himself. The movie was better than the usual oater. The language was clean, and the women were dressed. I don't mind a bit of nudity or a love scene, as long as it is significant to the character development and the plot, but I can do without the gratuitous scenes that plague contemporary films. Mostly I kept an eye on Benj, who seemed to withdraw inside himself as the movie progressed. By the time it was over, he was asleep on the sofa. I left him there, cleaned up the kitchen, and hit a textbook.

Benj awoke just before midnight and stumbled back to his apartment, aided by my turning him in the right direction once he was out my door. I watched him until he disappeared inside. I felt helpless afterwards. Sometimes there is just nothing that can be done.

Thursday afternoon—at which time Leah's schedule was supposed to be open—I rang her up and got a message tape. I said, "Pick up, Leah," to no avail. After throwing on a windbreaker against a mild chill that had cropped up from the south, I took the bus to the Foundry. As usual the office was empty save for Anthony. Opting out of coffee, I went to the restaurant next door and returned with a soda.

As they say, silence is golden. For the moment, I had nothing to say. The pile of magazines beckoned, and I selected the one I had started on a few days earlier. The articles seemed less appealing, and soon enough the magazine rejoined its companions.

I tried Leah again, with the same result.

"This is not something you can rush, Eric," Anthony said gently.

"I know. But sometimes I feel like I'm in a hurry. I don't know why."

"Of course you do."

"Of course I do," I sighed. "Anthony, I like...being with her. And I'm conflicted. She's a client, and I'm trying not to forget that. If she were anyone else, a classmate, say, I would already have asked her out. And gotten shot down, probably."

"Are you afraid of succumbing to temptation?" he asked.

The question left me dumbfounded. Until this very moment I had not thought of Leah as a temptation. If that were her status, then I ought to steel myself against her as anything but a client. Anthony's question begged another: what exactly did he mean by temptation?

Anthony laughed. "I see that the word has more than one connotation. Eric, if you want to ask her out, then do so. The search for self often requires subtlety. I'm sure you can help her, even if you are 'seeing' her."

I had a response almost ready, but my phone rang. I tokked it, and even before I could get a word out, Leah said, "I'm sorry, I'm so sorry. I saw the two missed calls. I didn't mean to make you worry."

"It's all right," I told her. "Everything's all right now."

Anthony had a half-smile on his face.

"Where are you?" I asked her, and she told me. I had to tune Anthony out. "Do you like manicotti?" I asked.

By the time Leah arrived at my apartment, I had the separate ingredients laid out on the counter and prepared for use. As I had done at her place, she now inspected mine. Windbreaker thrown over the back of the chair. Textbooks and handwritten notes cluttering the desktop. A sock I had missed. She browsed my bookcase, and gave herself several nods. Outfitted to absorb tomato sauce stains if necessary, she was wearing a well-worn turquoise jersey and dark, pre-torn jeans. Evidently she expected us to make a mess.

Once we were in the kitchen, her first words were, "Have you ever done manicotti before?"

"No. You?"

"I'm limited to spaghetti." She took a steadying breath. "Well, this should be interesting." Casually she looked around. "I don't see a recipe book."

"Manicotti is fairly straightforward."

She searched my face for several seconds. "You looked it up on the Internet. How do you know it's a good recipe?"

"Alimentary, my dear Watson."

Laughing, she tugged a large plastic bowl to a spot in front of her, and readied a rubber spatula. Ricotta, spinach, minced onion, an egg, mozzarella, and parmesan went into the bowl, and she began to combine the ingredients. I held a pepper mill over the bowl and ground perhaps a teaspoon of pepper into it.

"Now as to garlic powder," I said. "How garlic do you want to get?"

"It depends," she said. "Are we going to kiss?"

I was proud of myself for not missing a beat. "The recipe doesn't call for it," I said, and she smacked me with the spatula.

"You add the garlic, then," she instructed.

I dumped a rounded tablespoon of it into the mix, and she went to work in earnest on the ingredients. While she did that, I mixed the spaghetti sauce and water, and laid down a layer of it in the bottom of the casserole dish. The oven had already reached the 350° mark, and beeped its readiness. I opened the package of dry manicotti.

"Shouldn't those be boiled first?" she asked.

"It's hard to stuff a wet noodle. No, we fill them with that mixture. The sauce will soften them as they cook." I slid the casserole dish so that it rested on the counter between us. A few minutes later, a dozen manicotti lay in echelon in the dish. The filling in the seven Leah had prepared remained firmly inside, but some of the filling crumbled from mine. She poured the remainder of the sauce over the manicotti, and looked at me for directions.

"Top it with the rest of the mozzarella and parmesan," I said.

After she did that, I opened the oven door and slid the dish inside.

"Now what?" she asked.

"Now we wait for about fifty minutes or so."

It was the most natural thing in the world to take her hand and lead her to the sofa. We sat down, and suddenly I felt a little awkward. I had to find something to say, and quickly. She beat me to it.

"When I saw that I'd missed your calls," she said, "I-I found myself saddened, for reasons I really can't explain. I didn't expect you to call, but I'm glad you did. I seem to keep running away from you. You must have noticed."

"We were kind of thrown together into the mix," I pointed out. "It's not as if we had chosen of our own free will to be together."

"You're being kind."

I turned to face her. "Leah, I'm trying to help you. But there's...oh, God, I-I...how to say this? I'm glad you called back."

"I think I understand," she said softly.

Silence settled onto us like a warm fog. Soon enough, I decided that, client or no client, I was going to reach out to her. She met me halfway, and we held hands, neither of us looking at one another but with eyes straight ahead—at the stuffed chair and the DVD monitor on the table beside it. There was not enough time for a full movie, and in any event I had no desire to lose her hand. Again I wanted to speak, and again she spoke first.

"I wonder if God is watching us," she said, her voice barely audible.

"Always."

"Yeah. Where do you suppose He is right now?"

"Everywhere, Leah. Everywhere in the Universe. He is omnipresent."

"Even here?"

"Sundays we go to visit God in His house," I reminded her. "Of course He would visit me in my house. He is always welcome. Our house," I amended. "I mean—"

"I know what you mean, Eric. I guess I never really thought about it. But He is everywhere."

"He stands watch over you while you sleep," I told her. "He doesn't ask that you acknowledge this. His protection is a gift, a gift of His love. He does the same for eight billion of us."

"It's...difficult to conceive of, of that."

"God is full of mysteries. Most of them are beyond our comprehension, although every once in a while the

Holy Spirit shines a little light on some aspect or factor we should consider. For example, if you have a doubt, you might be nudged into thinking about it, thinking it through, to understand and know God just a little bit more. Knowledge of Him comes incrementally, and we'll never know it all."

She squeezed my hand, released it, and turned on the sofa toward me. "But that leads to the question of who we are to God."

"Maybe we are many things. Penitents, supplicants, worshippers. Even friends."

"You told me that before. Friends. But I don't understand how...how..."

"You pray to God, you worship Him, you adore Him. So talk to Him."

"I-I...but..."

In for a penny, I thought. "Leah, God is sitting over there in that chair."

"You...you really believe that, don't you?"

"More than believe. I know. Let's make the Sign of the Cross." Still puzzled, she made it and said the words with me.

"But why do we do that?" she asked.

"You learned it at St. Rita's. It's analogous to dialing a telephone. And now He has picked up. He doesn't have a message phone."

"You're serious."

I faced the chair. "I hope you like the manicotti, God," I said casually. "We had fun making it for you."

Leah was aghast. "You-you talk to Him like, like *that?*"

I did not respond directly. "As you see, I have a guest here this afternoon. Her name is Leah Hawthorne... well, I know you know that. You know everything. She helped with the manicotti, as you saw. In fact, she did hers better than I did mine. There's real talent there."

Leah sputtered. "But-but..."

"Thanks for helping me find the right recipe," I went on. "Actually, thanks for urging me to look up the recipes. I was just going to wing it."

Leah's eyes were wide now, and her breathing came rapid and shallow. Somewhat to my astonishment, she found her voice. "It's my first manicotti, too," she said, eyes narrowing at the chair. "I did the best I could." Quickly she apologized. "I'm sorry, I shouldn't squint at you. Please forgive me...whoa!"

"What's the matter?"

"I-I-I think I felt...something. A tiny touch of forgiveness. What does forgiveness feel like? But that's what it, it was. Eric...was it real? Was that real?"

"What do you believe, Leah?"

She sounded as if she wanted to cry. "Oh, God, I don't know," she wailed. "What am I supposed to believe?"

"That's not the question, Leah. What *do* you believe? Do you believe that God is sitting right over there, listening to you, reaching out to touch you when you are uncertain? Because we are not touching now, you and I. Yet you said you felt a touch, that of forgiveness. Forgiveness for a very minor offense, if it was an offense at all. So that touch had to have come from God. There's no other reasonable explanation. Leah, I would interpret that as being an invitation for you to keep talking to Him."

"And does this sort of thing happen to you?"

"More times than I can count. Each morning I go over my plans and hopes, my schedule—"

The stove binged. Fifty minutes were up. Interestingly, her eyes were filled with regret as we stood up.

The manicotti was delicious and I didn't pay much attention to it. My eyes kept darting to Leah across the table from me. I watched her eat; I heard her make quiet yummy sounds; I followed the movements of her hand, with the fork, from the manicotti to the mouth. Regarding the client aspect of her, she was starting to make a little progress. Her belief system had been jump-started, or defibrillated—really bad similes. *Clear!* But at the moment, she was not a client. She was my...my...

What would Anthony say now? Facing him, now, was going to be difficult. Almost as difficult as going to confession a year ago. But the words came easily. Anthony, I like Leah. No, I mean I really like Leah. Yes, she's a client, but this is not wrong, what I feel is not wrong, it can't be wrong.

"What's the matter?" Leah asked.

A quick thought arrived. "Not enough garlic," I said.

She considered that. "I think you're right. So next time..." She looked away, anywhere but at me. Her voice was a soft and hoarse whisper that floated like a cloud across the table. "Will there be a next time?" she wanted to know, braving a question she was afraid to ask.

I set my fork down; our eyes met. "Anthony wondered point blank whether I was 'seeing' you," I answered. "We were interrupted before I could say anything. Interrupted by you, as it happens. At the time, I'm not sure what my response would have been."

"And now?" she rushed in, breathless.

"I consider myself as 'seeing' you," I told her. "And I hope—"

"Yes!"

"...that you feel—"

"Yes!"

"...the same way."

"Yes, Eric."

"I'm glad. But it does mean that eventually we'll have to cut back on the garlic."

She threw a noodle at me; fortunately, it was empty, and spilled down my shirt.

"Leah..."

"Eric..."

"About finding yourself. We are now in a relationship with each other. That is now a part of our identity, of who we are."

She toyed with her fork at a glob of stuffing. "I think...I actually understand that. It's...I don't know. It's a step in the right direction for me. I feel...somehow, I feel a sense of relief. Because I am somebody to you, I'm somebody to me. But now I can be somebody to me, even if...well, no matter what."

"There's no way I can give up on you now, Leah," I said. "Not that there ever was."

"Thank you."

"For?"

"Just...thank you."

I got up from the table. "Leave the dishes and everything by the sink," I said. "I'll see to them later tonight."

"Movie?" she asked.

"What would you like?"

"Anything. A love story that ends well."

I gave that some thought. "*Charade*?"

She frowned. "I don't know that one. Assuming you mean a movie, that is."

"Mid Sixties," I told her. "Cary Grant, Audrey Hepburn. I got it for a dollar at the used bookstore."

"Um...I need to..."

I pointed. "Down the short hall and to the left. Don't go to the right, whatever you do."

That stopped her. "Why...why not?"

"Boris is in there."

"B-boris?"

"My anaconda. He's okay, he's still digesting that hog. But he doesn't like surprises."

"If you don't stop making me laugh, I'm going to wee right here."

After pretending to zip my mouth shut, I dug out the movie. The previews had finished by the time Leah sat down on the couch. She sat a little closer this time. By the end of the movie, my arm was around her shoulders, and she was snuggled against me.

The credits ended. The screen went blank.

"Leah?" I said, after a while.

"Yeah?"

"The last bus on that route stops here in about eleven minutes."

With a sigh she gently untangled herself. "All good things," she murmured, getting up.

I walked her out the door, and down the stairs, and outside into the cool night air. Slowly. Holding hands. We stood together, close enough for warmth. The bus came round the corner. Leah turned to me, and we hugged to the sound of air brakes hissing. To the sound of the door folding open. She turned, and started for the bottom step. She turned back around, and we kissed. Soft, soft lips that clung and held a promise of more. She had to have heard my heart, but what she said was, "Definitely needs more garlic. G'night, Eric."

And I was alone in the dark.

008

Friday I was not certain whether I wanted to fly or hide. Classes were a distraction from both possibilities. I hoped I wouldn't be called on, and that wish was granted. Dismissed from the second one, I fairly jetted to Anthony and the refuge he offered. I thought I might catch him alone, but my luck had run out. At least I had positioned my folding chair where the sunlight shone through the window. The warmth felt good on my back.

The new client was tall and angular, and might have played basketball at some point, though his black hair was now salt and pepper gray. His clothes were neat and dark, and vaguely like those of a mortician. But he was affable enough as he posed the problem. His house cat had gotten out and had not come back. He had tried the pound. He had tried the rescue shelters. He had posted photographs on telephone poles. He was almost in tears. Since his wife had passed away, the cat, whose name was Snookers, had been his only and constant companion. Finding a lost cat was not the sort of search that Anthony resolved. His streak of successes was about to come to an end.

But Anthony was not deterred. "Male cat?" he asked, and received a tight nod. "Neutered?"

"Yes, but is that important?" the man asked.

Anthony was noncommittal. "I'm simply gathering information, Mister Nordling. Normally something that is lost remains in one place until moved by some outside force. A live animal may be regarded as lost by its caretaker, but it does not itself feel lost, or confined to one location. Now, we have to assume that Snookers is alive and free."

"Oh, I hope so." He was almost in tears.

"And he got out through the back door, you said. Mister Nordling, you might check the Internet for sprays that smell like a cat in heat, and sp—"

"I told you: he is neutered."

"But Snookers doesn't know that. He may very well return to the back porch if you spray it. Of course, the drawback is that such a spray might attract a few dozen other cats. Still, it's a possibility worth considering."

Nordling cleared his throat. "It sounds like there's an alternative."

"There may be. There are also sprays that smell strongly of catnip. That has somewhat the same drawback as female musk, but at least the cats who show up will be laid back and cool."

Imagining a cat wearing shades and saying, "Far out," I fought back a laugh.

Nordling considered this. "That could work," he said at last. "Snookers loves catnip." He reached into his pocket. "What do I owe you?"

"Let me know if Snookers comes back, please."

"That's all?"

"If he comes back, that will be enough for me, sir."

"I will." Nordling nodded vigorously. "I will, indeed, and thank you."

After Nordling left, I took up his chair.

"You look as if you have something heavy on your mind, Eric," said Anthony.

"Yeah. And I'm not sure where to begin."

"At the beginning, of course."

I shook my head. "Not what I meant. You know the beginning. It's the middle that..." My heart seemed to stutter. I lost track of what I wanted to ask; I wasn't all that certain that I knew what to ask. Finally I blurted, "Anthony...are you a priest?"

A smile tickled his lips. "No. I had two years at the seminary, but the priesthood was not my calling." His eyes narrowed. "Are you thinking of confession? Of the sacramental seal of the confessional?"

"I guess so. I don't know."

"Eric...if that is your wish, nothing you tell me will leave this room, seal or no seal."

I withdrew a little. "Well, it's not...there has been no sin, only some..."

"Temptation?"

I nodded.

"Maybe you'd better start at the beginning," he said, and I found a quiet laugh.

I told him everything that had transpired during my date with Leah. I omitted nothing, including my thoughts. I also, with some trepidation, included a random and accidental observation.

"She had a toothbrush in her purse?" Anthony asked, after I had reached the point where Leah stepped onto the bus.

"I wasn't snooping. Like I said, the purse was open on the sofa, and the toothbrush was clearly visible."

"But she never said anything. She never hinted at anything."

"Well...no, she never did."

"So there could be a perfectly innocent explanation for the toothbrush in her purse."

The answer to that came readily enough. "But it was on top. As if she had put it in the purse at the last minute. Just in case."

Anthony almost laughed. "Those last three words you uttered. 'Just in case.' If your concern is in fact well-grounded, if you are correct in your assumption, then Leah would have said yes."

"Yeah. But the subject never came up."

Now he grinned. "You probably could have phrased that better." After I stopped laughing, he continued. "Eric, you've known Leah for two weeks. I accept that you are serious about her. Give it more time. Not that your interest would lessen, but that the two of you might well become more closely acquainted, to confirm what you obviously already feel in your heart."

Yeah, I thought, agreeing. "And the toothbrush?" I asked.

Anthony leaned forward, hands resting on the desktop. Given everything that had just transpired, I sensed a lecture coming. He had that look on his face. His opening words supported my expectation. But as it turned out, I was wrong. What I got was a parable of sorts.

"Sexual morality is the most difficult principle to adhere to," he told me. "Especially at your age. Especially once you've had a taste of immorality." Here his eyebrows arched a question at me.

I nodded knowingly. "I've...been with three girls. And I confessed this, and was forgiven. At the end of my Act of Contrition, I resolved to sin no more, and to avoid the near occasions of sin. Anthony, Jesus suffered death on the Cross because of the things I did. I can't do that anymore...I just can't...but Anthony, Leah is...well, she is."

Now he sat back, and took a long moment to consider what he was about to say. "Long ago, rather longer than I care to think about, I was eleven and twelve, and we lived in a housing tract on what was then the edge of a desert wilderness in Arizona. I explored, and caught lizards and snakes and trap-door spiders—they're a kind of tarantula—and avoided scorpions and the dangerous snakes."

"Something boys do," I said.

"Yes. Well, they used to do. Nowadays, sadly, they have other, more sedentary distractions. So, after a day or two I let my captives go. I fed them insects and watered them. And let them go. One day I caught a horned toad. They are a lot quicker than you'd think, but this one was shading himself from the sun, under a sheet of cardboard. That's where I would look first for creatures, but carefully, of course. When I lifted it, he was right there, and he never had a chance, though his legs kept moving even after I picked him up. I took him home. Carefully I laid him on his back on the palm of my hand, and gently rubbed a fingertip against his tummy, and he closed his eyes. He liked that.

"The undersides of most horned toads are yellow with little black dots. This one had the dots, but the underside was white, an eggshell white. Rather rare. Well, the next day, I let him go, as I always did. About a week later, I caught another horned toad. This one, however, was much easier to catch. He hardly put up any resistance at all. I got him home and put him in a box with some sand and grass. His tummy was white with black dots. I have no doubt, even today, that it was the same one I had caught the week before.

"He was easier to catch, Eric, because in the process of being caught the first time, he lost something. Maybe it was his confidence that he could escape danger. I don't know. But something made him weaker—it wasn't a visible injury—and easier to catch, now that he had first been caught.

"Sexual morality, once broken, is much like that horned toad, albeit in a different way. Now you know that sex feels good. You want more. And you know it's wrong. But it's easier now to...well..."

"Get laid," I put in. "But Anthony, that's not, definitely not, how I regard Leah."

"No, I know it isn't. But you have been caught, and you know what it feels like, and you are more attracted to sexual behavior than you might have been otherwise. Trust me, when you begin to approach my age, maintaining sexual morality becomes a lot easier." Here he chuckled, as if at some secret. "And Eric," he added quickly, "what I've told you is in no way a criticism or accusation, believe me. It's just the nature of human sexuality. So your integrity will have a more difficult test, because you have already had a taste. And if Leah has experienced...well, she may have the same difficulty.”

“I don't know,” I told him. “And I would never ask. Our life began the day we met. Whatever is past has been written, and is no longer a consideration.”

He nodded approvingly. “That may be the wisest statement I've heard you make. Borrowed, as it might have been, from the *Rubaiyat of Omar Khayyam.*”

“I've heard of it,” I said. “I've not read it. Leah has a copy in her bookcase.”

“But you may have heard quotes from it, including this one.” And he intoned:

> 'The Moving Finger writes; and having writ,
> Moves on: nor all thy Piety or Wit
> Shall lure it back to cancel half a line,
> Nor all thy Tears wash out a Word of it.'

But Eric, you can live the present well, and thus affect the future.”

“Oh,” I said. “That quote sounds familiar. And isn't there something about a loaf of bread and a jug of wine?”

“There is, indeed. Eric...give yourself and Leah time. You have plenty of that. You're young. This ‘assignment’ has certainly grown more complex, and in the growth of the relationship, of ‘seeing’ her, I think you may well discover that the relationship itself is at least a significant part of the resolution of her quest as a client.”

I could barely hear my own voice. “I hadn't considered that.”

He flashed a grin. “I had.”

Taken aback, I muttered, “For someone who was named for a saint, you certainly are devious.”

“Thank you. I try.”

The rest of the day flowed peacefully; it was a Friday, and most folks had other things to do besides misplace items. Like the Moving Finger, the sun moved on, and dimmed the office. I read; I pondered; I tried not to think of Leah, which meant she was never far from my thoughts. When I began to shift erratically in the stuffed chair, Anthony told me to go home.

In the apartment, after this and that, I tried several times without success to raise Leah on the phone. Although unconcerned—she might have been shopping, studying, visiting her parents, any number of things—the lack of a response left inside me a hollow place that not even the memory of her face and voice could fill. I tried to fill it with dinner, but everything tasted like manicotti stuffing with sauce.

Benj Davis saved me. He arrived just after the dishes were done. Brown eyes no longer wearing, and face animated, he announced the addition of five more hours a week to his job, at least for the next three weeks, after which Kellen Washingron's cracked forearm was expected to be sufficiently healed.

"He has employment insurance through his parents," Benj said, sprawling onto the sofa. I handed him a soda; he sobered after a couple sips. "I'm not happy that he can't work, of course. I happy that I can." He sniffed the air. "Was there a girl in here?"

He had to ask. "Yeah," I said. "Last night." I rolled my eyes; I was going to have to think more before I spoke.

Benj was all attention. "Ooooh?"

"Dinner and a movie," I said peevishly.

"Do I know her?"

"I doubt it."

"Are you going to see her again?" he asked.

The question slugged me. I hadn't even considered that, for whatever reason, we might not see each other. At the moment, I was absolutely certain that I could not bear it if she stayed away. And I had no idea why I felt that way.

"Hey," Benj worried. "I didn't mean anything by that."

"It's okay. Benj...yeah, we'll see each other again. And again."

"You're in love," he snickered.

Suddenly I did know why the thought of not seeing her was not to be countenanced. She was...she was The One. But now I had to wonder who I was to her.

As it turned out, I need not have worried.

009

I awoke to a vague impression of daylight through the curtains and to a slightly stronger impression of the aroma of brewed coffee. I was just awake enough to realize that I was still dreaming. This illusion was maintained until something landed on my bed hard enough to depress the mattress. I yelped, and tried to sit up.

Leah said, "Careful, or I'll spill your coffee."

My first action was to verify that I was fully under the top sheet and quilt. That brought a measure of relief. I managed to make it to a sitting position, and took the mug of coffee from her. Leah was dressed (another sigh of relief) in a pastel green suit that included pants and a vest, under the latter of which she had on a crisp white sleeveless blouse. She was seated half facing me—to confront me, she would have to climb onto the bed.

"Leah," I said, but I had too many questions lined up to be able to select just one.

"I was going to bang on your door," she said. "But your friend Benjamin has your spare key. You were sleeping so peacefully, not even snoring, so I did the coffee, and set up the waffle iron and the mix, and now here I am."

The questions remained in disarray. "Leah…"

"I thought you would be happy to see me. Maybe I should take that coffee back."

"No! No. Leah, I *am* happy to see you. I just…"

"That's better."

"I don't have a waffle iron," I said. "Or a waffle mix."

She looked as if she expected me to figure it out.

"I-I should get dressed."

"That might be for the best. I'll meet you in the living room."

Ten minutes later we were standing at the sofa. The waffle mix and iron were waiting for attention on the kitchen counter, but Leah had something else in mind as she bade me sit down, then joined me so that our bodies brushed against one another here and there. I looked a question at her.

"You told me that you talked with God every morning," she said. "You said that was how you began your day. Please tell me what you say to Him."

Of all the things she might have said, that was unexpected. The talk itself was personal, and yet it reflected my own search for identity. Perhaps it might aid her search as well.

We made the Signs of the Cross. In the silence that ensued, she regarded me expectantly. Our closeness lent an air of intimacy to what we were about to do, but it was spiritual and in no way sexual. Closer than this, we might never be.

I focused on the figure in the stuffed chair. "Good morning, God," I said, and diverted from my usual routine. "I've brought someone with me, as you see. Her name is Leah Hawthorne, and she is my girlfriend," she drew a sharp intake of breath at the word; I had surprised myself, saying it, "and she is trying to find you, and wanting to be found by you. She wants to know who she is.

"Thank you for a protected day yesterday, and please keep me—no, keep *us*—on the path today and give us the light to see it by. Please protect us from our past and from our mistakes, and our errors of omission and commission, from things we shouldn't have done and did, and should have done and didn't do. Please don't let anything catch up with us, and don't give us any reason to look back—"

Leah gasped. "The lesson of Lot's wife."

"I hadn't thought of that. But yes, you're right."

She looked contrite. "Sorry. I didn't mean..."

"It's quite all right, Leah." I turned to her and took her hand. "We're doing this together, even if it is I who knows most of the words." I returned my attention to the stuffed chair. "Please keep us headed in the right direction, doing good things, doing what we are supposed to be doing.

"Please watch over and protect my Mom and Dad..." I glanced at Leah.

"Please watch over and protect my Mom and Dad," she repeated. "And...and please see to my brother Micah, who is with you now."

"And our relatives and friends, our neighbors and neighborhoods, our homes. Please watch over and protect them all.

"Please forgive me...us our trespasses. Thank you for forgiving us our past, and now we need help with the present. We will always need those two sets of footprints, and sometimes the one set when it gets bad. Please help —"

She touched my arm. "Wait. What was that about footprints?"

"You haven't heard it? It's a story, possibly apocryphal, about a man reviewing his life while standing on the beach of life with God. He sees two sets of footprints leading back into the past, and knows that God was walking with him. But at several points in this trail of prints, there is only one set of footprints, and at those points the man's life was at its worst. He asked God how He could abandon him in his time of distress. And God said that it was at those times that He had carried the man."

Leah's sigh was the whisper of a gentle breeze through soft leaves. "Oh, my God, that's *beautiful*."

"Yes, it is." I fingered a few tears from her cheeks, her reaction to the story. A moment or two passed while she refocused, and I continued. "Please help us do all that we are supposed to do and can do, and be all that we are supposed to be and can be. Please raise us up, make us more than we can be. And please continue to be merciful to us sinners. As for everyone else, please clear our slates. I forgive them all their trespasses, and I ask that they forgive mine."

Leah squeezed my hand for pause. "I forgive them all their trespasses, too," she whispered. "And I ask that they forgive mine."

Again I turned to her. "Repeat after me now," I said, and paused for her after each sentence. "Please help me be patient, and tolerant, and resist temptation. Please guide my mind when I write and think and speak, and my body when I act. And if there's some task you'd like me to do, please let me know what it is, and I'll do it. Please help me not be lazy and not waste time and not put things off, just get things done and do good things.

"Thank you for being in our lives, God, and please stay in our lives." I drew my usual deep breath and sighed. My tone was more conversational when I resumed speaking. "I have a special request for Leah, God. She's on a journey of discovery. Please help her find what she is looking for. And watch over us the rest of the day. Stay with us, God. We'll be worth it."

A long and palpable silence followed between us. I scarcely heard her breathing. Her hand remained entwined with mine. I glanced at her, and saw a tear roll down her cheek. Her sigh was a burst of air. Her free hand pressed over her heart. Another and another tear fell, but no other sound did she make. She sat there, as if hovering. I had no idea what to say to her, or whether to say anything at all. I waited, and held her hand.

Without warning or word, Leah collapsed against me, sobbing. As we turned toward one another, our arms went around each other, and held on. Her chin rested on top of my shoulder, and a tear or two wound up on my own cheek. It took me a moment to realize that her weeping was peaceful, not sorrowful. I kept silent. This was her moment. She would speak when she was ready.

I kissed her just in front of her ear, and she pulled away. Moist blue eyes glowed at me. Her mouth worked, and she found some words.

"It's that simple?" she said, hushed. "You just talk to Him? Oh, Eric, I had the feeling He was listening."

"He was."

"He listened to us. To me. Oh, God. So I am...He is my God, He's..."

"He is your Creator, your Redeemer, and your Inspiration, Leah. You are his creature, you worship Him, and you honor Him with what you do."

"Even if...oh, I don't know. Even if I shop for groceries? Or serve food in the cafeteria? Or pass a test? No, you don't have to say it. I think I understand, now. I do whatever I can do, and keep God in my life. I don't have to think constantly of God; I do what I do, and do it well, and it is for Him that I do it. And that's the way it is. Oh, Eric, is that it, then?"

"There's always a little more to learn, Leah, but: yes, that's it."

She withdrew a little. "This was," she began, and stopped for words. "This was so, so intimate, and enlightening. I don't know what I see, yet, but it's there. It's like it's coming into focus." Our eyes met. "Is that how it was for you?"

"It was, and still is, a journey of discovery, and now and then a light goes on."

"I'm not...scared anymore."

"Time, Leah."

She nodded. "I know." Her eyes narrowed slightly. "Girlfriend?"

"It escaped before I could stop it; my heart overrode my tongue."

"Girlfriend?"

"Leah..."

"Just tell me," she whispered.

"Yes, Leah. Girlfriend."

We kissed. The temperature in the room shot up. Slowly we pulled away from one another. Her face was flushed; mine felt hot. I was able to resist only because I had spoken with Anthony the day before.

"Waffles," I said, apologetic.

"Waffles," she agreed.

They were the best waffles I'd ever eaten.

Leah had to leave after we cleaned the dishes and the counters. She was one of the few students who had a Saturday class. She meant to follow this with a bout of study.

"You could study here," I told her.

She shook her head. "We'd only wind up talking," she said. "Or something."

"Not necessarily. I have a story I'm working on."

Briefly she considered that. "I'll call you and let you know."

The mail arrived with some good news. A story of mine had been accepted by a professional magazine, and I now received a check for two hundred fifty dollars. Pending Monday and the bank, it went into the desk drawer. I felt like celebrating, but the person I wanted most to celebrate with was off studying. She might call; she might not. I trudged to the sofa and spilled onto it. A void filled me that not even a thought of Leah could fill. It began to occur to me yet again that I did not understand myself sometimes. I'd only known her for two weeks. It was not much of an argument. But an argument against what, exactly?

Fortunately, I had a default. "What am I doing, God? She's filling up all my empty spaces, and I don't know what it means. Oh, it means feelings for her, but she's not like any girl before...well, you know. You saw the toothbrush. I might have said a word—but I didn't. I do want her, but not...not like...she's special, and I cannot tell you why."

As always when I feel animated, my gestures punctuated my words.

"Girlfriend. That's an apt description. But what does it mean?"

A word or two drifted in from...somewhere.

"Yeah, I know, she and I are the ones who decide what it means. But we've yet to talk about it. It's too early to talk about it. We're just 'seeing' each other."

I sat up straight, and gesticulated.

"And you know what? I'm nervous. I know, I *know*, she's The One. I don't even know how I know that. Maybe it's a gift from you, knowing that. But we're twenty. Oh, it's not the age itself, it's the, I don't know, the immaturity, the need to finish at the university, to find a job, to...to... oh, I don't know, God. Leah and I, we each do our own dishes. We wash our own clothes. We cook our own meals." I chuckled. "Mostly we cook our own. That manicotti was...yeah. It was. And we made it together, Leah and I, and that made it taste even better. That means...something."

I gazed vacantly at the stuffed chair. Although the topic this time was different, the process was more or less the same. I'd had numerous conversations with God over the past year or so. Studies, work, questions, things I wonder or worry about now and then. But not about girls. A girl. A particular girl.

It occurred to me that what needed to happen next with us was to do some things together. A museum tour. And The City has a good zoo. Miniature golf. A walk in the park. And talking, talking. Light words. Beautiful sky today. Silly squirrels racing around that tree trunk. Someone walking a friendly dog. Watching a pick-up softball game at the park, and maybe even playing in it. Things to do.

It occurred to me that we had yet to broach our thoughts about the future. What were our majors and minors at The City University? What kind of work did we want to do after we graduated? Where have we been, travel-wise? Where would we like to go?

"God," I said. "Please, just show me..."

I sat back, and closed my eyes. Not in anticipation of an inspiration or a subtle hint, but to empty my mind for a bit of peace.

And I wondered whether Leah was having similar thoughts.

Around noon I got up from the sofa. I'd idled away enough time. Without much enthusiasm I decided to test the day. A rolled-up issue of an archeology magazine in my hand, I went outside to the little park across the street, and sat down on a bench dappled by sunlight through the foliage of a great oak tree. Turn the page, read the next paragraphs. See the photographs. Pages had to be held down in the breeze that blew up now and then.

But photographs of ancient ruins morphed into images of loveliness and intelligence. I had to look away. I should have brought with me a copy of *Newsweek*. A squirrel paused to stare at me. I should have brought peanuts as well, or maybe popcorn. That thought too was a mistake, for popcorn reminded me of a movie we had watched. The magazine now at my side, I gazed out into the trees until the combination of air and sunshine made me drowsy enough to go back to the apartment.

Toward evening I hit upon an idea: in the morning, when I went to attend Mass, I would arrive early and wait for Leah, so that we could attend together. I hoped that she would show up for that.

010

Rain awoke me in the morning, half an hour before the alarm went off. Weather offered a good excuse for not attending Mass, but those years had passed now. The driver of Number 11 saw me flag down the bus from the front porch of the apartment building, and I climbed aboard without much water attached. After closing the umbrella, I found a seat near the front. As the Number 11 also served the area where Leah lived, I wondered...and stopped wondering. It was too early for her. I'd have to meet her there.

Gradually the rain became a wall of water, and streamed along the street gutters to the drains. The driver took care at stops to pull as close to the curb as possible, to accommodate those boarding or disembarking. Windshield wipers swatted futilely at the rain, limiting visibility; he drove slowly. Our Lady of the Light came into bleary view. I tugged the cord, prepped the umbrella, and stepped off the bus and into the shower.

A mad dash got me to the foyer of the church. The doors were open—the overhang shielded the entrance from the rain. I kept watch, hoping to see Leah. A few other parishioners arrived, one soaked to the bone. An altar boy brought a towel for him. I glanced inside the church, and saw a small scattering of people. The rain was impeding attendance. I worried that Leah would choose not to brave the downpour. Perhaps, as I had done on two or three occasions, she would make up what she missed on Sunday by attending the Tuesday morning Mass. In a room off the foyer, Father Padraig was getting into his chasuble. The Mass was within a few minutes of starting. Deep breaths failed to ease my anxiety. Leah...

"Are you waiting for me?"

Her voice came from behind me. I spun around.

Her brown hair was sodden, and darkened to sepia under the blue and lemon scarf she was wearing. Her eyes held a bit of wonder at having spotted me. Her raincoat was open, and had stopped dripping. Under it hung a pale blue shift; blue and white loafers shod her feet, and left damp prints wherever she stepped.

A burst of joy cut off any flow of words I might have uttered. Bedraggled as she was, I found her a lovely sight to behold. My hand reached hers, and together side by side we entered the church and found a pew near the front. We freed our hands only to genuflect before entering the pew, and reclasped them after we seated ourselves. I leaned over and kissed the shoulder of her raincoat. She shrugged out of it, folded it, and laid it beside her.

Off to one side of the altar, a guitar started up. The opening hymn was *Amazing Grace*. We got to our feet. We both knew the words.

When the moment arrived to give one another the sign of peace, Leah and I hugged. We touched hands with those few worshippers nearest us—as I said, attendance was sparse. We took Communion. We sang the closing hymn: *You Raise Me Up*. Holding hands once more, we filed out of the church, pausing before Father Padraig to shake his hand and offer a few kind words.

The rain had stopped, having done its job. Leah and I had beaten it. We stepped out into a few rays of sunlight.

"I kept hoping you would show," she said, as she turned to me. Her eyes searched mine; I wondered what she saw. "I took an early bus."

"Have you had breakfast?" I asked her. She shook her head. "Someone left her waffle iron at my place, probably with ulterior motives."

"Probably," she agreed, and we made our way along the puddled sidewalk to the bus stop. She started to dip into a pocket of her raincoat for the fare, but I paid for both of us.

My apartment seemed brighter when we entered, an illusion I blamed on the company. Leah hung her raincoat over the bathtub while I dug out the waffle iron and the ingredients. Once again, as with the manicotti, we assembled breakfast together.

"Remember, only use the syrup once," I told her.

Her laughter was the sound of a silver wind chime. "At least there are no sausage links."

"I do have some, if you like."

She shook her head. "This is fine, Eric." Her chest rose and fell with a deep breath. "I was so hoping you would be there..."

"Backatcha."

"Yes. I could tell from the look on your face." She set her fork down. "Eric," she began, but other words failed to arrive. For a moment she looked lost. Then her eyes focused on me with intent. "Classes are almost over."

"I'm already boning up for the finals."

"Yeah. Me, too. And summer..."

"Summer?"

She hesitated, and for a moment her expression sobered. "Never mind right now. Eat your waffle."

"Leah..."

"I'll...tell you later."

There was nothing to do but accept and eat. Now I was worried. What had she been about to tell me? Her expression was unreadable, which I hoped meant that, whatever it was, it would not prove to be troublesome.

We finished breakfast with no further words between us, and cleaned up together before settling onto the sofa. An uneasy silence drooped over us. She was reluctant to tell me, and I did not want to press her. When I reached for her hand, she patted it but did not take it.

"I could put on some music," I said. "Something light."

She took a moment before responding. "No. Eric..." She turned to me. Her words flowed rapidly now, as if she were afraid of interruptions. "I'm...not going to be around for three weeks after finals. I'm going to Belize, as a sort of apprentice at an archeological dig in the Maya heartland. It's nothing noteworthy, just the excavation of what they think is a temple, but of course there are bound to be artifacts that need careful extraction and care. I'll be learning how to do some of that. I-I'll be leaving this coming Friday...I'm-I'm..."

I gave it my best face. "It's okay, Leah."

"It's what I've always wanted to do," she said, somewhat defensive.

"Your fourth class," I said. She frowned a question at me. "When you told me the classes you were taking this semester, I knew you left one out."

"I knew I would be absent," she said. "I didn't want Anthony to misinterpret my absence as giving up."

"He wouldn't have."

"I know that...now. I should have told him. I should have told you. Oh, Eric, I'm sorry. Not for going, but for the look on your face."

"Don't misinterpret that look, Leah. I'm stunned, that's all. But it's a reminder that we both have lives, we have futures, and dreams. They're as much a part of our lives as..." I glanced at the kitchen. "As breakfast together. Still, our plans for the future are not something we've talked about." I was unable to hide a note of dejection in my tone. "And I guess we won't discuss them for a while."

"Maybe I had better go..."

"No, Leah. That's why your search for yourself and meaning, and your relationship with God has made little progress. Every time you glimpse a possible answer, you turn away from it. You want the answers, but you're afraid of them. Now you're about to run away from me."

"That's...that's not fair, Eric."

"Isn't it? I said I was stunned, not upset, not annoyed. I've learned something more about you, something important. Your love of archeology. Not that it's important because I'm trying to help you find the answers to life's questions, but that it's important to me because I..." I closed my eyes for a moment, and hung my head. I knew what I really wanted to say, but it was too much and way too soon. Wasn't it? Wasn't it? I swallowed hard, and found my voice again. "So this is where your plans are, where your future is. That's what you see for yourself. My guess is that you're afraid I will spend less time with you now, because of what you perceive as a difference between us—a separation I had not expected. It doesn't occur to you that, stunned as I am, I might be happy for you. That I might be supportive. If I am disappointed, it is in that regard." I caught my breath. "I wish you had thought better of me, Leah." I let out a long sigh, and settled back in the sofa.

Beside me, still facing me, she began to weep. Now I did feel terrible. I had not meant to make her cry, but to understand herself. Doubts set in, worse than temptation, for I succumbed to them. Maybe Anthony had erred in assigning me this project. I was just an assistant, not a professional. I could well do more damage to her search than I knew.

Leah got up and trudged to the bathroom, returning with the raincoat draped over her arm. Her voice was stiff and unyielding. "You can keep the waffle iron while I'm gone," she said dully. "I won't...won't need it until I get back."

"Leah, don't..." But I could not complete that plea.

She made for the door and drew it open, and shut it ever so gently behind her, and did not look back.

011

Fittingly, it rained on Monday as well. The final in Medieval History was a two-hour exam with a choice of five out of ten essay questions and a selection of name identification, also in the essay format, but with shorter word-count requirements. I could not complain; I'd wanted to attend a university where you were expected to learn and think and apply, rather than fill out a computer card with responses to multiple choice and true/false. But my heart wasn't in it. I knew I did all right after I finished, but I was not satisfied with the quality of my responses, and I doubted that Professor Moore would be all that satisfied, either.

Rain continued to fall, letting up for a breather now and then. I arrived dripping at the Foundry, and waited just inside the doorway until the drainage had all but stopped. Anthony, intuitive as always, read something in my face that spoke beyond the weather. An abrupt gesture pointed me to the client's chair.

He got right to the point. "Did you and Leah have a disagreement?"

I bought a little time. "Did she say anything?"

He nodded to himself. "So the two of you did. Eric, do you want to talk about it?"

In the worst way, I realized. As before, I omitted nothing. After I finished, he sat back, fingers steepled, brown eyes gazing through me as if I weren't there. I knew what he was going to say. In any form of therapy, it's never a good idea for the therapist to become involved with the patient, in any form whatsoever. Psychology 101, which I'd taken last semester—so I should have known this. What had happened between Leah and me was the fault of my own involvement. It was not clear to me, however, just how that had affected the therapeutic relationship.

Anthony surprised me. "It seems possible to me," he said at last, "that your protest regarding the feelings you thought she imputed to you—upsettedness and annoyance—were not matched by your expression or body language." He raised a hand before I could argue. "I'm not saying you were upset or annoyed, although it would be understandable. But what you said and what you showed may have been two different things. But there is a ray of hope."

"And what is that?" I asked glumly.

"She'll be back for her waffle iron."

"It's not enough, Anthony." I got up and began to pace the office, muttering.

"What more is there?"

I paused in mid-step. "I-I don't know."

"You haven't told her." It was not a question.

Another pause, with a puzzled frown. "Told her what?"

"What you haven't told yourself, Eric."

I saw what he was getting at. "It's too soon."

"Is it? Truly? Because you can't tell her until you tell yourself. Until you acknowledge this to yourself, you won't be able to do what you should do to rectify this."

"You're talking in riddles," I growled. "You're not making sense."

"And you're proving my point. Deep inside, you do know what you have to do. First to yourself, then to her."

"She won't see me."

"You don't know that."

"She has finals before she leaves."

"She'll make time for you," Anthony assured me.

I threw up my hands. "How? How can you possibly know that?"

His smile in response was beatific. "Because she called me this morning and told me everything you just told me this afternoon." He got up and came to put his arm around my shoulders. "You know what to tell yourself, Eric."

Slowly I nodded. The words eased themselves out. "That I love her. That she is The One. But Anthony, it's... too soon. I'm twenty; so is she. The reality is that we have only just met. We know a lot about each other, yet we hardly know each other. How can I tell her that I'm certain? And what if she doesn't feel...I don't know. The same way?"

"You've never been in love," he said. "Maybe you've been in love with the idea of being in love. Maybe there was a bit of lust involved. But this time it's different, isn't it?"

"Yeah."

"Take your time. This takes time." He released my shoulders. "Your last final is Wednesday, right? That should give you time enough to pack."

"P-pack?" I felt my face contort. "What are you talking about?"

"I made the arrangements after she called," he explained. After reseating himself, he opened the center desk drawer. "You don't have a passport, and there's no time to get one from the U.S., so stand against that wall so I can take your picture." He tokked the phone, got up, and backed me against the wall. There was a faint flash. "You'll be traveling on a Vatican City diplomatic passport," he went on. "You'll be on the same flights with her. Dress coolly. Khakis, I should think. Light clothing. And be prepared for mosquitos. The expedition will have netting and lotion and repellent available. Wednesday afternoon, go see Doctor Hildy at the Rushman Clinic; she'll vaccinate you for Belize and give you a shot record." He brandished an envelope. "Your round-trip plane tickets, some cash, and a credit card. I'll have the passport for you tomorrow." He peered past me. "It's stopped raining, and I see part of a rainbow out there. That's a good sign."

Flabbergasted, I had to sit down. "Anthony..."

"I would suggest strongly that you take the waffle iron to Leah now, with the explanation that you couldn't wait to see her again."

My eyes felt huge. "She's *expecting* me?"

"Further deponent sayeth not," he said smugly.

"Does she...she know about this? About the tickets and...wait. This is an archeological project. I'm not registered with the expe—" I stared at him. "You didn't."

"I did."

"But...but...Anthony, all this must have cost..."

"I like ramen. So does Bishop Furrier," he said, and I had to laugh. He handed me the envelope. "The next bus stops in about a minute, Eric. And don't look so surprised at any of this. I find things. It's a gift, as you know. Apart, the two of you are lost. Together, you are found. You go find her, so St. Anthony and I can chalk up yet another victory."

I saw the bus pull up outside and stop, and wait. I had no idea whether Anthony had arranged that as well.

My heartbeat sounded louder than the knock on her door. Leah scarcely gave me time for worried anticipation. The door opened as if she had been standing on the other side of it, waiting, waiting. I held out the waffle iron, which she took absently and set on a table by the doorway. In the very next instant she was in my arms, knocking me back a step as she murmured incomprehensibly. A few words burbled into my ear. Words I should have said to her first. I wasted no time in responding in like manner.

"I love you, Leah."

Her lips moved against the side of my neck. "I'm glad that's settled."

"I've been an idiot."

"So have I. I was scared, Eric. You were right. I flee from possible answers."

"That's over now."

I felt her nod. "Maybe we should adjourn to my sofa," she suggested.

I needed no further invitation.

On the sofa, after she brought out sodas and placed them on the coffee table, we simply sat together, turned slightly toward one another, somewhat clumsily holding onto each other. She was wearing a sleeveless white blouse, the top two buttons open to reveal a silver crucifix, and a green, blue, and yellow plaid skirt, and brown sandals. Her toenails were unpainted. I took in all this, because I was trying to ignore the warmth of her against me. Without much success.

Finally Leah pulled away enough to see my face. "He called to tell me you were on the way," she said. "He also told me about the expedition."

"It's...not too late for me to cancel, if—"

"Don't you dare! Eric, I know now who I am to you and who you are to me. There's much more to be learned, but I know enough to see this through. I have that part of my identity. I have only one major question left: who am I to God? When I find that answer," she touched my cheek, "with your help, I will be found. Eric...never let me go."

"Never."

"You've already declared yourself, as have I," she went on. "I came to understand my feelings for you after I left, and on the bus, and especially after I arrived home to an empty apartment. I knew you were right. I fled your apartment. I could have stayed. We could have talked this out."

"It's all right now, Leah."

She studied my face, and I saw its reflection in her sapphire eyes. "Anthony hinted that you might tell me something else."

"I can't tell you how I know this, Leah, because I don't know myself." I gathered the words and freed them. "You are The One."

"Oh, yes, yes," she breathed. "I know exactly what you mean. Eric, you are my One. I knew this as soon as I returned home, but I did not have the words." She was crying, but tears of joy. "Eric: together."

We touched foreheads, and sat there like that for uncounted time. A minute, several of them, without interruption. We had opened the same door. The path led forward, and was wide enough for the two of us. I could not see the end of it. Maybe there was a light there. The only thing that mattered was that we were headed toward it.

Lost for words, I pulled back. She said, "I recalled seeing the stack of magazines in your apartment. But you're not taking Archeology."

"Given my major, maybe I should."

She laughed. "Maybe?

"I'll register this summer, after we get back."

"You don't have to, because of me."

"A trade, then. I'll take Archeology, if you'll take Medieval History."

"Deal."

"How's your finals schedule?"

"Humanities and English Comp tomorrow, Algebra Wednesday.

"Ouch."

Confidence filled her smile. "I'll ace them. Now," she added, and squeezed my hand.

"I hate to say this, but we'd both better hit the books."

For a long moment she searched my face. "Eric... help me find out who I am to God. I need that in my life as much as I need you in it. Maybe even more than. Anthony told me you once had the same questions, the same... doubts. You found your answers. Help me to find mine."

"I didn't find all the answers, Leah," I cautioned. "Not even enough of them. The knowledge of God is...it fills a hogshead, and I only have two rounded teaspoons of it. That may be all I get."

"I trust you."

And that brought tears to my own eyes.

Again silence reigned. I broke it, diverting to our textbooks. We had priorities, after all. It hurt to release her hands. She threw them around me, and we kissed, softly, gently. Lips clinging together. Despite the light contact, there was more passion in this than you see on television or in movies. Shaken, I had to pull away.

"I'd...better go," I whispered hoarsely.

"Wed-Wednesday," she said. "Afternoon."

"Yeah."

But there was something in her eyes that told me she still had a secret. Given the mood, and the feelings, I decided against inquiring after it. At the door—she wisely remained on the sofa—I gave her a long look, and shut it gently behind me.

The bus back was superfluous; I could have flown.

012

Final exams the next day. In the afternoon I picked up my passport. Anthony told me that technically I was still on the job, Leah being my assignment, and therefore I would be paid. Anxious to know how Leah did on her exams, I wanted to leave, but instead I found myself asking about the source of Anthony's funds. It was a nosy question, and none of my business, but he explained readily and amiably after I sat down in the client's chair.

"Officially I would be addressed as Brother Anthony," he began. "I am a Franciscan monk of the Third Order Secular. Such as we do not withdraw from the world, but we teach, and we perform works of charity and social service. But that, of course, does not explain the money."

"Maybe you don't have to tell me, Anthony."

"It's quite all right. It's not something I talk about, but in this case it's worth making an exception. Eric, I was born to an inheritance of a little over twenty-six million dollars. It was all mine, and at first I had no idea what I wanted to do with it. I thought of many irresponsible things. I could own a collection of Maseratis, or buy an island in the Aegean, or live in a penthouse. In a way, I was somewhat like you and Leah, in that I was lost, and did not know what to do. But I had something else going for me: my religious beliefs. I could not envision Jesus approving of my car collection or island refuge or living at the top of the world. A vehicle and a place to live would have to satisfy me instead. Upon reflection—I had by this time obtained a college degree and attended the seminary—I realized that I was being called to do is what I'm doing now. To help people. For me, that takes the form of finding things," here he smiled, "empowered, I have long believed, by the patron saint of things lost. But my training also includes guidance, especially subtle guidance. This in fact is what God does—a nudge now and then to keep you on the path. In my poor way, I try to emulate that.

"So I gave away the money, in a manner of speaking. I set up a trust fund for the use of the diocese here in The City. I can draw on it as needed, as can the diocese. We coordinate with one another. For example—and this goes no further, Eric—a needy family might find themselves in possession of a turkey for Thanksgiving or a ham for Christmas.

"This trust fund is how your trip to Belize was financed. It is fitting, because in addition to your personal interest in the trip," here he smiled once more, "you do have that assignment I gave you. And before you ask, yes, I thought putting you with Leah Hawthorne would be, let's say, good for both of you. You've been where she is—searching for yourself and God. You've found some answers. In time, I know you'll find more. I think Leah will accompany you on this journey through life."

"Match-maker," I chided gently.

"It's not set yet," he reminded me. "You two still have to decide on the course of your lives, and whether you want to journey together. That entails more discussion than I daresay you've given it."

Anthony was right about that, and I told him so.

"Both of you still have some growing, some maturation, to do. But I will tell you this, Eric: I believe it is going to work out for the two of you. Just remember to take your time. You two can always turn to me if you have questions."

So now I knew the secret of Anthony's expense account. He had placed himself in the service of God. The money was an occasional means, but not an end in itself. I was sure there was more that he was not telling me, especially about serving God and about his charity work. Along the way, I expected to find out what that service meant. I expected Leah and I to find out what it meant.

In the meantime, the Chemistry Lab final exam awaited.

On Wednesday afternoon Leah and I issued sighs of relief. The semester was over. The grades would be posted on Thursday. In the meantime, there was preparation and packing to do. Unfortunately, these were activities we were unable to do together. So we took a little time out by sitting on the sofa in her living room and breathing those sighs of relief, and making small talk. She suggested I stay for dinner. Some mention was made of sharing a broiled Porterhouse steak in celebration. I was assigned potato-mashing and salad-tossing duties. But the celebration had to wait.

We had adjourned to the sofa, as I said, and sitting close to one another but not quite touching. We had established the beginning of one relationship—ours. At the moment, it was not the time to approach the relationship with God. Lost in her own thoughts, Leah said nothing. In the worst way I wanted to know what she was thinking. But something told me that this was not the time to break into her silence. I sat, and watched her out of the corner of my eye, and waited.

Finally she said, "I don't want you to study archeology for my sake, Eric. You have set your course in history, so you told me." She turned to me. Her eyes glistened in the light from overhead, and I knew she was on the verge of tears. "Please don't abandon that for me."

"Archeology is a form of history, Leah," I pointed out. "I'm not lost in it; other than reading magazine articles, I simply haven't studied it. But I find it very interesting, and now I have a reason to pursue those studies. Leah, in some ways, I'm still lost, but I have a direction to travel now. To travel with you. I'm not giving up history; I'm adding archeology."

She searched my face. "You're sure about this?"

"If you will have me along."

A hard sigh came from her, and for a mad moment I thought I had upset her. A scant second later, she was in my arms, and we were stretched out on the sofa. My hands trembled, touching her face, her arms. Lying on our sides, we kissed. I knew what could happen next, as if it were foreordained. As much as I wanted to, I couldn't take the next move.

Her voice shook. "Eric..."

"Leah. I-I...it's not that I...Leah, I promised God. I've been forgiven my past transgressions. I'm not going back to who I was." Which I knew would be easier said than done.

I expected almost any reaction but that trace of a smile on her lips. "Then you'll have to be strong, my love. Because you see, there are no more tents. You'll have to sleep in mine."

"Besides, I suppose we'll be too busy..."

She nodded. "That could well be. So we'll learn how to work together."

"Which segues to that steak and the side dishes."

We sat up. I sighed. "Leah..."

"Yeah. Me, too."

And that was where we left it.

Just before dark, I took the bus back to the apartment. Temptation resisted. I did not know whether to laugh or cry. My own sofa beckoned, and it reminded me that Leah could be sitting there, waiting. I sat down hard, and looked at the stuffed chair.

"God, not that it matters, but nobody would believe what I just did. Or rather, didn't do. Anthony cautioned me to take time." A notion wandered across my mind, and I snagged it. "Yeah, I've known other girls. They were temporary, even fleeting. And they are past. Leah is—oh, please let this be so—permanent. So I want everything to be right." A light laugh followed. "And I could use a little help with this from you."

A distraction was needed. I went to the bedroom to finish packing.

013

Mostly we slept on the flights to Belize City, where the only major airport is located. There was no direct flight, and we changed planes three times. As advertised, Leah had aced her finals and finished with straight A's. I had three A's and a B, the latter in Medieval History, which was annoying. We talked about the Gulf, which despite all the islands was mostly bluish water, without features. Coming into Belize City, we flew over the second longest barrier reef on the planet. We disembarked into hot and humid air, and broke out in a sweat almost immediately.

We boarded a local flight inland to Belmopan. The Belize River flows just to the north of that city, and our dig site was located about a mile north of the river. Three jeeps traveling over rugged terrain and roads of dried mud took us and our equipment to the site. That trip took almost as long as the flight from Miami; asphalt apparently was sorely lacking in the country. A few very colorful birds protested our passing, and one of them left a deposit on the hood of our jeep. Welcome to Belize.

The site had yet to reveal its name, and so it was referred to as The Site. We, which is to say, the expedition, arrived in late afternoon and set up camp about fifty yards west of the digs, in a clearing that had already been checked for ruins, with negative results. The expedition numbered seven of us, including Doctor Miguel Ramos, who headed it and who spoke contemporary Mayan. Four of us were students, and the other two were graduate assistants. One other expedition was in the area, working on the same site, but we had only sporadic contact with them. Leah suggested that there was a note of competitiveness between the two groups; as we were in the jungle, and the site had only been reported a year ago, the ruins had only begun to be uncovered and explored. In some ways the entire area felt spooky, as if it were the backdrop to a B-grade horror movie. When I told Leah this, she pointed out that such a movie, called *The Ruins*, had already been done. But she was certain that it had not been filmed in this area. Both her hands were behind her when she told me this, and I suspected that her fingers were crossed.

Hygiene was arranged about ten yards south of the campsite, where sheets had been erected for privacy and narrow trenches had already been dug. There were also a couple of makeshift showers, watered by the indigenous Mayan assistants, but it was not expected that we use them daily. We could clean up more thoroughly after we returned to the States. Leah and I had brought four sets of outer clothing, including the ones we were wearing; again, indigenous support saw to laundry. While there were jaguars and snakes in the country, the Mayans had arranged a watch schedule for the night, armed with rifles; however, we were assured that the likelihood of an encounter was minimal. But the word "minimal" went undefined.

Evening meals were simple, warmed in pots over open fires whose beds had been well-cleared of all possible flammable debris. Though not *Gibson's* of Chicago, the food was palatable. To the far west, past the jungles of Guatemala, the sun sank toward the horizon, and I almost expected to hear a hiss as it struck the ocean. Darkness, when it fell, was total save for the fire, which was extinguished by one of the graduate assistants after we had gained our tents and sealed them against flying and terrestrial pests.

Slipping into our light sleeping bags, Leah and I collided several times—elbows, knees, hands, feet—as we drew off our outer garments and folded them at the head of our beds. The tent was spacious enough, but barely. As we started to roll away from each other, I changed my mind, turned her back to me, and we kissed goodnight—

risking not much more than a peck before turning away again. Respiration slowed, and the next thing I knew, someone was banging a pot, and it was time for breakfast and then for work.

Leah was assigned to scratch at something embedded in the dirt next to a quarried stone, while I was sent to accompany one of the graduate assistants to explore an opening in a wall of stone that led to the interior, possibly of a temple. Inside were known to be faded paintings. The assistant—name of Tara Wolfe—would take the photographs, while I would set the lighting. Wolfe—call me Tara, please—was twenty-three, and working on her Master's thesis pursuant to eventual doctoral studies, and had been published professionally three times already. Attired in khaki shirt and shorts and sturdy black boots, all she needed was a white pith helmet and a quirt to fit the stereotypical archeologist. She kept her brown hair very short, practically little more than a cap. In the boots, she probably cleared five-foot-three, and without them might have weighed an even hundred pounds. Already, because of that height, she had explained to me that I might take a photo or two myself of some of the art higher up, which she wanted shot dead-on. The hand-held camera and the recording camera were simple enough to operate. All I had to do was follow instructions and, at times, fetch electrolytic beverages, as it was going to be even hotter inside.

As it turned out, the opening led into a chamber some eight feet wide and high, and ten deep. Only one wall contained art, in the form of glyphs. These had faded over time, but the recordings—film and stills—would be digitally enhanced in the laboratory so that the colors received clearer definition. Our job was to make the recordings.

"Can you read these glyphs?" I asked Tara.

Her gray eyes looked dubious. "I'm working on it," she said. "I recognize a few of them, not enough to make sense of a translation. Let me have that spot over here, please. How did you meet Leah?"

Unprepared for the inquiry, I hesitated, which earned me a questioning glance from her. "We share an interest in philosophy and religion," I said, hoping the response was general enough. "I myself have only read archeological magazines, but I've already enrolled for next semester."

"Eric McCleod," she said, pronouncing it correctly as MacCloud. "I saw your name on the student rolls. You'll be in my Archeology 101." She pointed at a clutch of glyphs at my eye level. "Get the spot on those, and take a still. Then I'll shoot some film in horizontal sweeps over this wall, and you match me with the spot."

As I moved into position, my boot lip caught on something, and I kept myself upright by hands against the bare part of the art wall. "What?" I said, and glanced back. Tara did the same.

Something dark protruded about half an inch from the floor of the chamber. It vaguely resembled a finger, and I prayed that it was not. With the spot on it, I dropped to a knee.

"Don't touch it," cautioned Tara, now also on a knee, hers bare. She took the spotlight from me and began to examine it from various angles.

"What is it?"

Tara shook her head. "Metal, I think. That could make it an artifact." She dug out her radio, and asked for Leah to join us with her tool set. She told her not to bother with a theodolite, a suggestion that said I had a whole new vocabulary to learn.

Tara stood up. The back of her wrist drew a sheen of sweat from her brow. "You get to watch your girlfriend at work. I don't want to step around much until we've determined what this is. There's no telling how deeply it's embedded, and I'd like to know if there are any more trinkets in the floor."

Leah arrived focused. I got no more than a nod of greeting as she set to work. First a flat-edged skim trowel, carefully applied to lift a thin layer of dirt from the surface. This she did all around the "finger" of metal. Repeat and rinse. After a very quiet hour or so, she had scraped or brushed the dirt down about three inches. The finger curved further into the floor, and she had to widen the hole to account for the bend. I made two trips for drinks, and after the second one Leah sat back and took a few breaths, and wiped her face on her shirt sleeve.

"Nice work," said Tara.

"I think it's gold," said Leah.

"It looks smooth," I added.

"The way it's curved," said Tara, "it could be a torc of some kind. Leah, keep at it. Eric, I think you'd better fetch Doctor Ramos. He'll probably want us to preserve this site until a fuller exploration can be made."

It was difficult to dash off in that heat and humidity, but I managed to walk fast enough. Ramos was on his knees at a small dig, with a magnifying glass in his left hand. He was a short man, maybe four inches taller than Tara, with wide dark eyes that protruded as if he had been born with the desire to take a closer look. The armpits and back of his light blue shirt were darker as he looked up at me. I explained what Tara had said.

"A torc?" he asked, getting to his feet. Beads of sweat dripped from the tip of his nose.

"It could be."

He said nothing further, but did dash off. I took my time returning, and when I arrived he was watching Leah's work very carefully, brushing for her while she scraped with the skimming trowel. The least important of the four at the moment, I took the spotlight from Tara and aimed it at the little excavation. There was nothing else to do but watch the work.

Another hour passed, while all of us dripped onto the chamber floor. By this time, Leah had managed to expose the other end of the torc, about seven inches down. At this point, Ramos halted the digging, took out a tape measure, and estimated that the torc—for now it definitely was—would have fitted around a size fifteen neck. But the rest of the curved part awaited exposure.

At this point Dave Barber, the other graduate assistant, hallooed from the chamber entrance and announced the arrival of the air van, a vehicle whose A/C would allow us to cool a little during the weltering hours of the day.

Ramos said, tersely and a little disappointed, "Let's take a break."

It would be nice to say that our first day had met with great archeological success, but in fact we were unable to finish extracting the torc. Leah's careful skimming of layers of dirt had turned up a more delicate artifact. She managed to expose one full side of it—it appeared to be a cube about two inches on a side—and portions of two others before we had to break for dinner and cleanup. The full side bore a single glyph, and one of the other two sides was exposed enough to reveal a portion of another glyph. Nobody, including Doctor Ramos, had any idea what this object might be. I suggested it was a die for casting, and this was met with odd and tolerant smiles, except from Leah, who looked thoughtful.

In our sleeping bags that night, we listened to rain spatter the tent. It had a minimal but welcome cooling effect. Leah resumed her pensive expression as she gazed at me in the dim light of a candle I had just lit. When I asked her about it, she hesitated before answering.

"That was not a bad idea you had," she told me. "Early dice are known in Asia and Europe, but not in Mesoamerica. Of course, that does not mean that what we found is a die, but I would not dismiss the possibility out of hand, either."

"So why…" I started, and was unable to complete the question, because I did not know what to ask.

Leah did know. "This is Doctor Ramos's dig," she said. "He would want the privilege of discovery. Your observation, if accurate, took that away. Some archeologists are jealous of their prerogatives. Probably at the moment, he's trying to figure out two things. One, is this really a die? And two, how can he bypass you and claim the credit for it?"

"Leah, I don't really care…"

"But he doesn't know that. And you should care at least a little. Again, if accurate, that was a brilliant insight." She paused a moment for reflection. "It's also probably a bit galling that a newcomer, virtually ignorant of archeology, came up with the possibility."

"So you're saying I should keep my mouth shut?"

"I'm saying, 'well done,' my love."

She leaned closer and kissed me, and I lost track of what I wanted to say. We settled on, "Good night," and let the rain lull us to sleep.

For the next eight days, the dig passed more or less like this. Lots of tedious work with little apparently accomplished. The torc proved to be a gold torc, with some engravings along the outer curve that needed analysis back in the lab. The cube was, yes, a cube, with glyphs on all six sides; no one had a clue what it might have been used for, and no one mentioned the possibility of a die. We also turned up some turquoise amulets, several shards of broken pottery, a damaged but still serviceable vase or container, possibly for water, and a small drinking cup in the bottom of which was a blackened residue that Ramos said might be cacao.

And each evening, it rained. This soothed and mildly cooled us, and despite the damp and the mud made bearable the digging—a verb that apparently included every activity. By the ninth day we were exhausted and ready to go home.

It was on the last leg of the flight home that I felt the first intestinal rumblings. By the time we landed, I was ready for the hospital. Arriving at it quickly, there was where I stayed.

014

The diagnosis was amoebic dysentery. In my case, I had some intestinal bleeding. I was placed on IVs and given antibiotics (metronidazole, whatever that was) and saline. And I missed Leah. She'd had to file reports of her activities with the expedition, and that took priority. I understood that; still, her absence was depressing. Worse, because my hemoglobin count was going down, I was jabbed every four hours for a blood sample. Which meant I could get very little sleep, because every two hours or so the nurse tech also came to check blood pressure and oxygenation.

By the evening of the second day, misery had set in. I hadn't seen Leah. I hadn't heard from her. She hadn't visited. I was disconsolate. I tried reaching Anthony without success. The end of the world felt like it was setting in. Each time the nurse tech came for blood, I cringed. The veins in my elbow ached in anticipation of another jab. I hated amoebas. I was too weak and too tired even to grouch at the techs. They kept me alive on tasteless orange jello. I craved a hamburger, large fries, and a chocolate shake. I wanted manicotti. I wanted to make manicotti with Leah. I wanted to see Leah. But no Leah, and no Anthony. I'd been deserted, abandoned, forsaken. Tears formed for no reason, and would not stop. I could barely sleep.

The third day was, if anything, worse. I lay in bed. It was too narrow to be comfortable. The nurse's aides came in to change the sheets. I went to the bathroom. I was still bleeding. It looked worse than it was, but all I could think of was that it looked worse. I missed Leah. I missed Anthony. One of the nurse techs was named Destiny. She smiled at me. It did not help. I wanted a smile from someone else, who wasn't there, who had forgotten all about me.

In the afternoon, weary and low and despondent, my thoughts drifted to some lines from a song. The title of it was *You Raise Me Up*. The first verse starts out with how miserable the singer is. The singer is down and oh so weary; troubles burden the heart; and the last line...

The last line of the first verse went, "Until you come and sit awhile with me." That person would be Jesus, or perhaps God. I don't know which Person of the triune, and at the moment, I didn't care. I was thinking, yeah, right.

But something urged me to extend my arm along the mattress, and hold out my hand. And I felt the bed shift as if someone had just sat down. Someone who took that hand and held it. Someone who said nothing at all, nor did I speak. There was only the comfort of His hand with mine. Nothing more than that.

Fog began slowly to lift, and with it, despair. I felt lighter. The hand kept hold of mine. Maybe for a quarter of an hour. To this day, I don't know for how long. Nor does the time spent matter much. I could barely keep my eyes open. And eventually, He released my hand, and left.

Maybe half an hour later, I got up and went to the bathroom. There was no bleeding whatsoever. None. Nothing at all.

And I knew precisely what had happened. I wept, cried, sobbed. All for joy, not for sorrow. I had been...I knew, and know now...I had been touched. I had been cured.

The doctors agreed about the cure (I did not tell them of the visitation, for it was too personal, too private). They said I was being discharged. I could go home. Oh, joy, I could sleep in my own bed, amid familiar surroundings, with no one to come in and jab my elbow or take my blood pressure or affix another IV. I called Anthony, and finally, finally, reached him and told him where I was. He came to get me. He took me home. He saw that I was all right.

And he saw that Leah was waiting inside the apartment for me.

I totally broke down. My knees sagged. She hugged me, and took me to bed, and laid me down there. Breathing came so easily. Relief and comfort were mine again. All I could see was her. Anthony, behind her, waved goodbye; we would speak later.

After the door closed, my voice croaked, unused these past three days. "Leah, I..."

"Hush." On the verge of tears herself, she sat down on the edge of the bed. "I'm so sorry. I had to file...oh, God, I should have told them to stuff the reports, because you were...oh, God, I'm so sorry, Eric." She held my hand as I looked up into her glistening sapphire eyes. "Please, please, forgive me. I will never do this again. I will never leave you alone in your hour of need. I love you. You are my—"

I managed to cover her mouth. She would have said, "Boyfriend," or perhaps, "My love." But now that was incomplete, it had to be incomplete, there was no other way, not now, not now. There was no other life possible.

"Leah," I said. "When it's time, after we graduate, will you marry me?"

Her "Yes!" came breathlessly and immediately.

She stretched out alongside me. And held me. We needed no words. I felt her breathing, her chest slowly rising and falling with each breath she took. And for the first time in three days, I went to sleep and slept soundly.

I awoke to those eyes. The curtains open, I could see that outside night had fallen. Leah had been watching over me. I had an idea that someone else had been watching over me. God, Jesus, guardian angel, and the angel lying alongside me. I closed my eyes, and moments later opened them. She was still there. So, I just knew, were They.

She helped me sit up. Unnecessarily, for I felt fine, just fine. She scooted up so that she was sitting beside me. My hand in hers.

"Hungry?" she asked.

"For you."

"Backatcha. Can you walk?"

"Leah, at this moment, I can fly."

She slipped her feet to the floor and got up. Her hand made a desultory gesture. "You probably need to use the... I'll meet you at the table. Tomato basil soup, to start you off. I'll...watch. Eric, I have missed you so much. I'm so sorry."

"Nothing to forgive, Leah," I said, and got up. "You're here."

"Where I should be. Where I hope to be, always." She gave me a gentle shove. "Go. Just go."

The soup was hot. I burned my tongue. It didn't matter. But I had a worry. "How are you getting home?" I asked her.

"I am home."

"Leah, no..."

She reached out for my hand. "I know. I know. We won't. As hard as it will be, we have to do this right...oh, my God, did I just say...that?" Her face turned a beautiful, floral pink.

We both laughed, I for the first time in days. The soup had cooled sufficiently by the time we stopped.

"No dinner for you?" I asked her.

"I'll make a sandwich. We'll watch a movie. We'll have a popcorn fight. I'll sleep on the sofa. I'm staying here with you, Eric, at least for tonight. Not for...any loving. We'll get there by and by. But...I need you. I need to be near you. I don't know what the solution is. We'll work it out. But not tonight. Tonight, we rest, we sleep. The morning will be brighter."

And so it was.

015

"I do have reports to finish," Leah told me at breakfast—waffles, of course. "I'll go this afternoon. I should be back by five or so. I'll call if it's going to be much later, but I doubt that it will."

"We have to talk," I mumbled between bites.

"We certainly do. After we do the dishes. I'll wash, you rinse and dry."

The dishes done, we repaired to the sofa with mugs of coffee. But the topic of discussion was not ourselves. She opened abruptly, as if she had to get this out before she lost her courage.

The subject she had chosen was God. She believed in God; she believed God, what He had said in the Scriptures and in Tradition. Faith was less a question for her than I thought it would be. She had faith; but faith in whom? Who was God, and what was she to Him and He to her? Certainly the deepest of questions. At least she knew how to pose it; she knew what it was that she did not know. Finished for the moment, she looked to me for a response, one sepia eyebrow raised over eyes so reflective that I could see my face in them.

In posing her questions, Leah had touched upon the difficult question: how much of God can human beings know? This was a matter that Anthony, or Father Padraig, was far more qualified to address than I. What did I know? I was still on the never-ending journey myself.

I began slowly, gathering myself along the way.

"Leah, it is beyond us human beings to fully know God. He is the Creator of the Universe, and we are His creatures. Everything we see is His creation. He is infinitely more than His creation, while in comparison we are...I don't know. Photons? Neutrinos? Quarks?" A smile chased across my mouth. "In your case, a charm quark.

So we have to be satisfied with what little we can know of God."

And it struck me.

"I told you this before. Think of all the information about God as filling the inside of a barrel, a fifty-five gallon drum. I know, it's a poor metaphor, but…anyway, of that information, what we get to know during our lives is equal to about two rounded teaspoons."

She barked a laugh at the unexpected reminder.

"Sometimes, if we're fortunate or intuitive enough, we get a few granules for a third teaspoon." I took her hand, for no better reason than I liked taking her hand. "But the important bits of knowledge are beliefs, are of faith. We believe in God. We hear and obey God's revealed word. We understand that sin is a rejection of God, of God's Will. We know God loves us. We know Jesus has saved us. But we still have to behave ourselves. We still serve God, we obey His will. Yes, it really is this simple. Difficult, at times, but not all that complicated.

"To serve God, we live—or try to live—our lives well. We each have a calling. Yours is archeology. Mine is history. Anthony's is finding things. Candy's may be working at the candy store. If we choose to follow that calling…well, first we have to learn what our calling is… but if we follow it, we serve God. We glorify Him. We follow God's word. There are the Commandments, of course. No murders, thefts, covetings, adulteries, false gods, curses, and so on. But what did Jesus say about commandments? Thou shalt love thy God with thy whole heart. And just as great: thou shalt love thy neighbor as thyself. In other words, love God, and treat other people as you would treat yourself. That's it, Leah. That's our lot in life."

"You're scary," said Leah.

Taken aback, I could only gape at her.

"You make it sound so clear," she explained. "So easy."

"Oh, it's anything but easy," I replied. "There are always speed bumps. Call them temptations. I wish I had his car. Or he needs a punch in the nose."

"Or I'd love to take him to bed?" she tried.

I nodded vigorously. "Definitely a temptation. I just...Leah, I want this to be right for us."

She touched my arm. Her hand scalded me. "I know. I understand. I want it to be right. It would be easy to surrender. One day, Eric, the day we are married, you will surrender. And so will I, that I promise you."

For a minute and more there was nothing I could say. Or there was nothing I trusted myself to say. Some temptations are...difficult to fight.

"Knowing God," she said, "I get that. We can only know so little. But...how, how can you love God? You can't even see Him. You can't...oh, I don't know." Frustrated, she dragged rigid fingers through her hair.

"Oh, Leah. All right, you have reports to file. It's okay, I understand. I'll pick you up at your place this afternoon at, let's say, half past six. Dress for a mild chill."

She blinked a "What?" at me.

"I can borrow Candy's helmet," I told her, and pulled her to her feet. A kiss ended the discussion for the moment. "Good luck. See you this evening."

"Eric..."

"Hush," I said. "Surprise."

Although I prefer public transportation, there are times when a bit of transportational independence is useful. Thus, for such occasions, I have an older Honda PCX with a sidecar, the latter being useful for carrying groceries and other shopping. I got it out of the garage behind the complex, borrowed Candy's helmet for Leah, and took off for Leah's apartment. Parking outside, I tokked her to come down. She did, she stopped, she stared. I waved, and motioned her to the sidecar.

She paused before getting in. "Seriously."

"You won't believe the gas mileage." I handed her the helmet, and noted that she knew how to don it and strap it. Motorbike, yes, but not her first rodeo. I had no worries about her in the sidecar.

The exhaust was just loud enough to prevent conversation without becoming obnoxious. We rode through The City toward the western edge of town, but unanticipated circumstances delayed our arrival there. As we approached an intersection with a traffic light, one car ran the red and struck another. The impact crushed the passenger-side door of the struck vehicle, so that only the jaws-of-life could open it.

"We have to stop," we said in unison, horrified.

The driver at fault got out of his vehicle and fled the scene. There was no question of us chasing him down; the injured came first. The other driver, a shaken middle-aged man, staggered around to the passenger side, and threw up his hands in helplessness and fear. I reached the smashed door and immediately saw the impossibility of opening it. Inside sat a woman in her forties, still in her seat belt, which might have to be cut before she could be extracted. The airbags had failed to deploy. Blood was streaming down the left side of her face; she had been cut by window glass. A heavy bruise was also forming on her left cheekbone, and she had bitten her lip during the crash. There was something wrong with her left arm, as she was holding it at a bad angle. She turned terror-filled eyes at me and Leah.

Mentally I threw up my hands. What could I do? "Are you all right?" I asked, with merciless banality.

Leah touched my arm, a caution to me to sound more sympathetic. Already she had the phone out and had tokked 9-1-1. I listened to her give the event and the location, and her name and mine as witnesses. The police wanted her to stay on the line, but she rang off. Questions had, for the moment, become irrelevant.

"I'm dying," croaked the woman.

I doubted that, but had no basis for doing so.

"I haven't..." Now she gasped. "I haven't been baptized," she wailed. "I'm going to die, and I haven't... haven't been..."

I felt as I had on the hospital bed, weary and helpless. But the word of an idea came to me, and I grabbed at it like a drowning man at a straw. "Leah, there's a bottle of drinking water in the sidecar."

She dashed off before I finished the last three words.

Carefully I used the hem of my jersey to remove some of the spiderwebbed window glass so I could safely reach inside the car. The woman watched with eyes now glazed. As far as I could tell, she was not fading, so much as she was terribly frightened. Leah nudged me with the Evian bottle.

Taking it, I asked the woman. "What's your name?"

She spoke raggedly. "Jo...Jolena. Jolena Morgan."

"I have to baptize you as a Catholic," I told her. "Is that okay?"

"Yes," she cried. "I'm dying."

"All right. I need to baptize you in a saint's name. The name of a saint to help guide you through life. Someone to intercede for you." I gave her the first name I could think of: my mother's. "What about Margaret?"

She nodded. I did not know the exact words. I knew there was something about Satan's pomps and works. I had to improvise. Surely such would be satisfactory. God knew my heart, and Leah's. And the woman's.

Over her bloody forehead I began to dribble glacier water. It cleansed away the blood to expose a short and shallow gash. I tried to sound solemn, without much success, for my voice was tight. "I baptize thee Margaret, in the Name of the Father and of the Son and of the Holy Spirit." I emptied the bottle, hoping it was enough. "Say 'Amen,' Margaret."

She did so. In the distance, sirens wailed. I spoke quickly. "Jolena, as soon as you can, go to Our Lady of the Light and see Father Padraig. Tell him what happened, tell him what I did here. Tell him my name: Eric McCleod. He'll make it all okay."

I tugged on Leah's arm. "I'd rather not answer questions right now," I said, and drew her through the few people that had gathered around. "The police will know where to find us, if they need us."

A minute later, we were putting along the avenue again.

"Can you do that?" Leah asked, over the exhaust. "Baptize people?"

"I don't know. I was trying to ease her worries. She's not going to die, as far as I can see."

"Oh, Eric..."

"That's why I sent her to Father Padraig. Whatever I did wrong, he can fix it."

She thought about that. "Where are we going?"

"There's a park up ahead, just outside The City limits," I told her. "It has an oak tree that is over three hundred years old."

"I-I don't understand. A tree? You're taking me to see a tree? I mean..."

"Wait and see."

In ten minutes, we reached the park. Few people were about. I docked the Honda near the Sherwood Oak, as it was called. The trunk was a good five feet in diameter, and even at this late hour offered some shade. Two squirrels chased, and Leah laughed at them. She said something about whose acorn this was. Three children played some incomprehensible game with a colorful ball. Parents, evidently, watched them and watched over them. These things and more I pointed out to Leah in passing. She had noticed them as well.

The sun continued to sink. God's crayons began to color the horizon and lower sky. Reds, yes, but pinks too, and salmons, lilacs, purples, smudges of indefinable hues, all across the horizon. Leah and I gazed at the sunset and held hands, looking, just looking. The sky darkened, and the sunset faded. Venus, the Evening Star, emerged, brighter than Sirius. Other points of distant light poured through holes in the sky poked by giant remote fingers. There was the constellation Leo and its bright star Regulus. Up there the great triangle of Vega, Deneb, and Altair. Of the three, the intrinsically brightest was Deneb, which would have rivaled the sun were it as close to us as Sirius. And that great gout of cream spreading across the sky was our galaxy, just one of billions, billions!—the Milky Way.

The oak tree was a dark shadow, looming but not frightening, rather a haven against the darkness because you knew what it was—a refuge for squirrels, wrens, sparrows, chipmunks, God's creatures all, all.

I held her hand, and pointed here and there with my other. There, and there, and there. Stars, planets, trees, and oh, the last remnants of that sunset!

"Leah," I whispered in the shadows, "you asked me a question this morning. Do you recall it?"

I felt her nod against my shoulder. "I asked how you can love God."

"And I answer you now, my love, with what we have seen this evening: How can you not?"

Leah dropped to her knees on the grass beside me, and wept. I joined her there, and we worshipped each in our own way.

And I heard her whisper, "My Lord and my God."

Bed awaited me after I dropped her off and I returned to my apartment. A drink of water, a bit of toast and butter. I wasn't hungry, and I doubted that Leah was, for we had expended emotional energy at the great oak, in a burst of discovery and realization for her, a powerful reminder for me, and we were now exhausted. Though she had said nothing, I had the feeling that she had found the answers she had sought. I flipped through magazines for a while, without much interest, so shaken were we by the overall experience.

In the dark, I disrobed and climbed into bed. A bit of trembling told me two things: we wanted each other in that way, and we were going to wait, it mattered not the difficulty in that waiting. But I knew, as I drifted off to sleep, that we were going to have to do something about this.

That "something" came sooner than we expected.

016

In the morning, after breakfast—Leah came over and I did up cheese omelets and unconfused sausage links—we sat on the sofa and recited the daily talk with God. Leah said it relaxed her soul; I understood that well. Then she broached an idea that was fraught with temptation but made sense.

"Should we move in together, do you think?" she asked.

My brain said, "No," and I ignored it. But I could think of no other response.

She drove ahead. "I would move in here. I pay more rent, so we'd save money if we were together here. The same goes for utilities. That's the practical side. Food for two is not that much more expensive than food for one." Smiling, she glanced around meaningfully. "I have less to move than you do. And yes, I know I'm avoiding The question. But that has already been answered. We wait."

Leah made sense. I told her that.

"But?" she said.

Still I had no answer.

"There's something else," Leah went on. "I'd like you to meet my parents. Over dinner, let's say. I want to go talk with them later this morning."

That at least evoked a response. "Are we ready for this?"

"My love, we are going to be married. We're ready, ready or not."

She had a point. We got up. "You go talk," I told her. "I'll do the dishes."

After she left and caught the bus, I gave it fifteen minutes. I had something more important than dirty dishes to see to. The Number 17 came by, and I took it downtown. What I wanted drained my debit card down to the rest of the month's groceries. That task completed, there was nothing left to do but wait until she got back.

Leah returned just after noon, looking somber. "It's on for this evening at six," she told me, as she flopped down on the sofa.

I handed her a soda. "So what's the matter?"

She shook her head, took a sip, and set the bottle on the coffee table. "I'm...not sure. And I'm not sure I want to, I don't know, predispose you."

I knew that tone. "You're not sure they approve."

Sighing, she gazed up at me. "So well you know me." Abruptly she flashed a wicked grin. "But I still have some surprises left."

I sat down beside her. "It's funny you should say that." I dug out the little black velvet box and opened it. "Leah, will you marry me?"

"Oh, my God, yes! Oh, Eric! It's beautiful!"

"It's just a simple diamond. It's all I could afford. I hope you like ramen." I slipped it onto her third finger left hand.

"No," she said firmly. "It's not 'just a diamond.' It's my rock. It's my engagement ring. We're officially official now."

I showed her the matching pair of simple rings of white gold. "One of these goes with that, one day, when—"

Whatever else I was going to say, she stopped with her lips. When we finally came up for air, we leaned back and gazed across the room at the stuffed chair in peace and silent gratitude, and eventually caught our breath.

"It's two o'clock," said Leah, nudging me, the moment coming to a pause. "I should head back to my place for something to wear."

"It takes you that long?"

"It takes an hour just to dry my hair."

"I stand rebuked."

"You stand loved." She kissed my cheek. "Pick me up at half past five."

At the appointed time, dressed in black slacks and a black and blue checked flannel shirt, and a pair of brown loafers usually reserved for Mass, I putted the Honda to her apartment, tokked her phone, and waited. Leah did not merely step outside. She made an appearance at the top of the steps. The same white cotton frock with borders of bright blue flowers now draped from her resolute shoulders as it had the first day we encountered one another in the Foundry. The hem of the frock swirled around her lower thighs as she descended the steps one by one, as if she were well aware that I was watching her. Which I was. In that moment, she was a living, walking piece of fine art, demanding a viewing and an understanding of what, exactly, the future was to hold for me, for us. A hand over my heart calmed it as I watched her approach the Honda. As she accepted Candy's helmet and put it on, tucking the brown ponytail out of the way. As the diamond sparkled in the late sunlight. As she climbed into the sidecar, knowing that she gave me a little better view of her legs in doing so. As she seated herself girt for war with her parents, if that was how it would be writ. As her firm and radiant expression now announced to the world that she, *we*, meant to win and indeed had already won.

As a nod to me got the Honda started up.

I followed her directions, and we arrived in the driveway circle ten minutes early. Her parents' home was set back a good fifty yards from the street, and was more manor than house. Gabled roof with two dormers like great triangular eyes. Trim of dark wood along the lower half of the front wall, and fronted by well-kept lilac shrubs that had been dead-headed for the year. Great bay window to the left of the front door, with indoor plants on the shelf; I half expected to see a furry white cat sitting beside the corn plant. Another, smaller window to the right that might give onto a study or library. The upper half of the house was bright white with a pastel blue trim along the eaves. I parked the Honda behind a glistening black Chrysler Imperial, this year's model, that rested under a maple tree that had to be a century old. We walked purposefully to the front door, which Leah opened without knocking, and announced us.

From her father, Addison, Leah received a hug and I a firm handshake. Anticipating a bone-crusher, I slipped my hand forward to clutch at his wrist, to minimize the damage. This earned me an odd look. From her mother, Barbara, who immediately noticed the ring, Leah received a hug and I a stitched smile of greeting. Well, I had been warned.

There was no tour of the house, no attempt to impress me with wealth. In a way, that failure was more expressive; they did not feel the need to flaunt what they had. As we moved to the dining room, I took a few meditative breaths, for I was approaching this encounter the wrong way—give them a chance, try to work things out. I was in control of my actions, not theirs. I hoped the attitude would work.

The table was laid out nicely on a lacy tablecloth by the middle-aged woman in a black uniform fronted by an immaculate white apron bordered by lace. She stood to one side, awaiting orders, while we seated ourselves, Barbara opposite me, Leah opposite her father. Leah smiled, while I managed a flicker of one; neither gesture was returned. At a signal from Addison, the maid lifted the silver cover of a silver platter to release the rich aroma of a prime rib roast. Light from the overhead chandelier sparkled off the shiny metal as she set the cover on a smaller table. Another cover, over a ceramic bowl, shielded the mashed potatoes from cooler air. A silver ewer contained pale brown gravy. Broccoli with cheese sauce completed the culinary array.

Addison, armed with an electric knife, started to carve the roast. I took Leah's hand; she in turn reached for her mother's, but failed to grasp it; Addison's hands were full. Undaunted, Leah and I recited a food blessing. At least the Hawthornes paused long enough to respect the prayer, but it was clear that such an invocation was rarely heard in this house.

After her father finished carving the roast—which was done to a medium rare turn—the maid and a man in a butler's uniform began to serve the food. No one touched their plate until the serving was completed. Barbara signaled the maid for attention.

"Colas for our guests," she said, as if Leah and I needed reminding of our ages. "Addison and I will have the Chusclan."

"Very good, Mum," said the maid, and departed with the butler to fetch the beverage order.

Wow, I thought; otherwise, I was temporarily bereft of words. Still, I said, "This all looks delicious. Thanks very much for having me over." I garnered two quick perfunctory nods in reply. The drinks arrived—the butler filled the wine flutes while the maid popped the tops on the cans. With fork and steak knife, Addison began to address a slice of roast, a signal to the others to begin eating.

Several bites later, her father's first question to me was exceedingly polite, and I knew an ulterior motive lay behind it. "Leah tells us you're majoring in history."

"Medieval, primarily, sir," I replied.

"Is there much money in that?"

Bang! Score one for him. Leah's eyes held a silent plea for me.

"Enough to live on, sir. Sometimes more. There are all sorts of job opportunities for someone with a degree in history. Teaching, of course, and research for publication; museum displays, especially anthropological displays, require factual statements of origin, which in turn have to be researched; corporate human resource offices; tourism and tour guides. Sir, there's any number of opportunities, in this country and overseas."

"Have you been overseas?" asked Barbara. "Besides your recent trip to Belize. With our daughter," she added, two seconds too late.

"Not yet, ma'am. But we will." I gave the pronoun just a nudge of emphasis.

"On a motorbike?" asked Addison, pointedly.

"No, sir. Oh, the Honda does get great mileage. Probably three or four times that of, say, a Chrysler."

Leah wiped her lips with a napkin. Behind it, she mouthed to me, "Good one."

"We'd rent or lease a car once we arrived."

Barbara turned to Leah. "You'd travel with him?"

"Of course, Mom. Wherever he can find a job in history, I can find one in archeology. The two sciences are related, you know."

"I did not realize that history was a science," was her mother's rejoinder.

"Any system of knowledge is a science, ma'am. There are hard sciences, such as physics, and soft ones, such as sociology. Or history." After a small toast of gratitude, I took a sip of soda from the can. "In addition, history requires at least a working knowledge of hard sciences. For example, Newton's discoveries regarding gravitation—"

"Yes, yes, we know all that," her father said impatiently. "We are far more concerned about your support for Leah. Have you, for instance, medical insurance that would cover her?"

I tried the mashed potatoes. As expected, they were perfect, as was the gravy. I gave the maid a little nod of appreciation, which seemed to shock her. But a faint smile did tickle the corners of her mouth.

"Not yet, sir," I replied. "I do have full insurance where I work, but I won't be able to add Leah until after we're married."

"After graduation, I understand," said her mother. Something in her tone told me she did not expect me to graduate.

"That's the plan," I said, around another chunk of roast.

"And after you graduate," asked Addison, "will you continue working for this, this Foundry?"

"Probably for a while, sir, until I find other employment. I could also go on to graduate school."

"And live on what?" he asked.

I shrugged. "I'll continue working; we both will. And there are always student loans and grants available. I don't see a problem, sir."

Her father laid down his fork. "I'm afraid I do see one. I see several. Let me ask you this: when was the last time you ate a meal like this?"

"Dad!" cried Leah.

I gathered some of that courage that had brought me to Confession and back to God. "Whether you are referring to the meal, sir, or to the ill-mannered behavior of the hosts, I can truthfully say: never." I stood up and held out my hand. I did not have to invite Leah by word of mouth.

Oh, she did not blink, my love did not hesitate for a nanosecond. She rose, and we turned, spines like girders, and hand in hand we walked out the door. Her father shouted something that the closing door sealed off. We made straight for the Honda, donned helmets, and rode away.

Leah's tears had dried by the time we gained my apartment. As soon as we were inside, she fell into my arms. Fortunately, I had anticipated such an impact, and rocked only one step backward. She rubbed her nose against my shoulder.

"I'm so sorry," she pleaded. "I-I...I did not, did not expect them to...to..."

A finger under her chin tilted her head back. "And what great sin have you committed?"

A wan smile flickered on her lips and died there. "I know one I would like to commit with you, right now, right now."

"So would I," I told her. "But let's give it a few more days to marinate."

Her eyes grew huge, each filled with a star sapphire that reflected my face. "A few more days? *Only* a few more *days*?"

Our bodies found the sofa. She drew her legs up under her; I had to look away. We turned to face one another, and joined hands.

"I think your dad shouted something about your financial support," I said.

"He's going to withdraw it. It doesn't matter. I'm going to apply for a grant or a loan for next semester."

"When is your rent up?"

"Saturday."

"Three days. We'll have to hurry."

"Wh-what? Why? Eric, what are you thinking?"

"We move you in here before then," I said. "Day after tomorrow, you pack."

Her eyes searched mine. "But...but I have a few bits of furniture," she said. "The Honda won't...won't..."

"Hush. Benj has a pickup. If we can't fit it in that, you don't need it."

She laughed. "I suppose you mean my bed."

"Did you want to bring it?"

In response, she leaned forward to be kissed. "It would only gather dust," she told me. "But we can use the bedding. Eric?"

"Yeah?"

"Are we really going to do this?"

"Surely you don't have doubts."

"Go lie down on the bed, mister. I'll show you what value doubts have with me."

"A few more days, Leah."

She blinked. "I think I know what you're thinking. Eric, I haven't even thought about a wedding gown."

"What you're wearing is fine. It's you."

"And a tuxedo for you?"

"I'll wear a bolo tie with the flannel shirt. I think I have one somewhere."

A breath eased from her as she nodded her head in acceptance.

"May I suggest a quiet, private wedding?" I asked.

"Yes. Yes, of course. What did you have in mind?"

"In that little chapel at the side of the church."

"Oh, yes!"

"Tomorrow, we go get the marriage license, and stop by the Foundry for a consultation and counseling with Anthony. After that, we'll go see Father Padraig, who will counsel us and do the ceremony. I'll ask Anthony to be Best Man. Who do you want for Maid of Honor?"

"I-I don't know."

"How about Candy? She'd love it."

"And I have to return her helmet. All right, I'll ask her tomorrow."

"Benj has a camera for photos, and his truck for our transportation. We'll need two witnesses, but that will be Benj and Candy."

"And...and our honeymoon? Where do we go for that?"

"I was thinking our bedroom."

She prodded my chest with a hard finger. "I like the way you think, sir."

"In the meantime, I'd better sleep on the sofa."

"Why?"

"Leah, I-I...oh, God, I want you. But I want more for this to be right."

"Everything being right is just as important to me, my love," she said softly. "But there is more to sleeping together than the loving. I want...I need now...to know that you are close by when I sleep."

"I know that feeling."

"I understand the sofa. Or maybe I should go back to my place, and avoid the near occasions of sin, right?" She tagged my arm. "Go pick out a movie. I'll do the popcorn."

"Make two batches," I told her. "Candy just came home, and Benj is already home. Hey, you could stay with Candy; just ask her. So: which movie?"

"I don't know. Something light and idiotic."

"*Howard the Duck*?"

"Maybe three batches, then."

The movie and gathering was, as I had hoped, a time to firm up plans for the wedding. Benj asked for gas money for the pickup, and Candy gave the helmet back to Leah as a wedding present, saying, "But I would like to borrow it now and then."

We talked and laughed. I don't recall much of the movie, or of anything else. Leah and I needed the unwinding. In the end, after cleaning up the popcorn on the sofa and carpet, we were exhausted but with minds eased now by the setting of our plans. After a kiss or two, she left the apartment to go stay with Candy. Before I closed my eyes, I asked my parents for their blessing, and asked them to attend...in spirit. So much had become clear to me, in so little time. Anthony says it happens that way when you are open to possibilities.

017

The details of the move and the preparation went as expected: lifting, sweating, taking the stairs down and back up, filling out license forms. In addition to a small and quiet wedding in the chapel, we planned a small and quiet reception in the Foundry. Leah left a courtesy message on her parents' phone, not expecting any reply. Candy arranged for a cake from the candy store—they baked on request. Benj got a full tank of gas for transportation, including on the wedding day. Anthony was pleased to be asked to be Best Man, although as we discovered later, he was far more than that. Candy had a bride's-maid dress, unused because that wedding was canceled, and it still fit her. Anthony rang up Father Padraig, and confirmed with him that he would perform the ceremony in the chapel *provided that* the next day Leah and I showed up for Mass to be feted during the sermon. This seemed a reasonable request, easy to fulfill, as we had accustomed ourselves to weekly attendance.

Leah and I set up bookshelves in the honored tradition of college students, which meant arranging wooden planks across concrete blocks for shelving. Her end table and the lamp on it were welcome additions to the sofa. Her clothes went on the left side of the closet, mine on the right. The armoire was the heaviest piece of furniture she brought with her. Life is just one thing after another. Maybe Mark Twain, who knew a lot about Life, said that. He knew whereof he spoke.

On Saturday all the pieces fell snugly into place. I don't know why. There's Murphy's Law to deal with. But Leah and I arrived (separately, I in Candy's car) at the chapel at the appointed time—two in the afternoon. I had even found my bolo tie, with a spot of help from Anthony (it had fallen behind my dresser). I gave the wedding rings to Anthony, who was doubling as ring-bearer (call me Frodo today, he said, lightening the already-festive mood). He took up a position behind me and to my right.

Father Padraig set on the little altar a chalice covered with a white veil, with enough consecrated wafers for the gathering. Already he was dressed for the ceremony, in white chasuble, cincture, liturgical stole, and cassock. Benj had a recording ready—Pachelbel's *Canon in D*, the arrangement by VioDance, with Rebeca Sanchez on violin—which Leah and I had selected after listening to several possibilities. As the "aisle" from the chapel entrance to the altar was maybe fifteen feet long, Leah would have to walk slowly (no) or walk stately to join me before Father Padraig and wait for the music to end (yes). As this particular piece had brought tears to our eyes in appreciation of beauty, we were more than willing to wait.

As Leah had to be given away, that task too fell to Anthony. He stepped from the chapel and waited for Leah to arrive with Candy. Father Padraig's smile of reassurance relaxed me. Like all brides and grooms, I wanted this to go right. A simple wedding ceremony; how complicated could it be?

When Anthony returned inside alone, I began to fear a complication. What if Leah...but no, I could not believe she would fail to show. Something might have happened. A delay in traffic. Her veil blown away. Two o'clock passed. Where was she? Time and time again, I glanced back. I was not supposed to see the bride until she stood beside me. I was risking a break with that tradition by turning around. Deep breaths, deep breaths. Good air in through the nose, bad air out through the mouth. What was Anthony doing back inside? Where was Leah? Why had Anthony's face become inscrutable?

Twelve minutes after two. The front door of the church creaked opened. I dared not look back and break with tradition. We'd gone to a lot of trouble, and fought back even more temptation, so that this moment would be right. Anthony was still standing behind me. Benj started playing the *Canon.* The music made me tear up, as I knew it would. But what...what...?

I waited. Waited. I sensed her coming up beside me. Not for me to look at. I was brave, courageous, determined. Father Padraig began his "Dearly Beloved" speech. Anthony was still standing there. Maybe Benj had been delegated to give away the bride. As long as she was given away, the ceremony would be right and just.

Father Padraig reached the part where he said, "Who is to give away the bride?"

"That would be me," said Addison Hawthorne, behind me.

I spun around. Addison raised his hand for peace. Beside him stood Barbara. Both were attired in church casual clothing, appropriate to the simple ceremony in progress. "I apologize to you both for our behavior," he said. "My only excuse is that we want what is best for Leah. After speaking with Mister Lost, we came to see that you, Eric, are best for her."

Under the veil, Leah's tears flowed; they matched mine.

Someone said something, probably Father Padraig. My attention fully on Leah, I did not catch the words.

Father Padraig tried again. "Do you take this woman..."

I'm sure he said the rest. When he stopped speaking, I said, "Yes, I do take her."

He repeated the question to Leah. I had ears only for her response. "Oh, God, yes, I do, I do."

Leah and I received Communion, as did Anthony. She and I bowed our heads in silent prayer.

Father Padraig pronounced us husband and wife. I lifted Leah's veil and we kissed. We did not wait for him to say we might.

There were hugs all around. I didn't keep track. I wasn't tracking very well anyway. Neither was Leah.

Nor do I recall much of the trip to the Foundry. It had been set up for the reception. Already Candy's promised cake—chocolate fudge with white frosting and our names in rich blue lettering—rested on the end table beside the desk, awaiting attention. We gathered inside, with Leah's parents nearby, and gazed longingly at that cake.

The front door opened behind us. Addison said, "Excuse me, but I hope I'm doing this right. I know you wanted a simple wedding and reception, so I...well, I...I ordered a bit of catering. I hope pizza is appropriate," he finished, as a man carried a stack of three flat cardboard boxes into the office and deposited them on the stuffed chair. "Please tell me it is."

Leah stepped to him and kissed him on the cheek. "You did just fine, Dad," she told him. "You and Mom. Thank you."

Leah and I cut the cake, and stuffed pieces into each other's mouths, making the traditional mess. Benj, who had been shooting photos with his phone, continued shooting, all candid shots except for three or four poses. The food was an odd combination of tomato sauce, mozzarella cheese, chocolate cake, and vanilla frosting. I don't recall tasting any of it.

I just...I just...hoped the pictures would tell us what happened.

Leah and I were alive. We had found each other, and she—like me before her—had found God. We were set for life, however it would be writ.

018

Stories never really end, so yes, there is more to this one.

Candy had already presented her wedding gift, the helmet. Benj's gifts were his transportation and his photographs. As the reception ended, my in-laws called us aside to hand me a white business envelope.

"We didn't know what you needed," Addison explained. "But there is always a useful standby."

I opened the envelope. It contained a check made out to me for ten grand.

"If you need more," he said. "If you need anything at all, just ask. Please?"

"And come around for dinner," said Barbara. "Whenever you have a chance."

"We will," Leah told them, and they departed after hugs.

Father Padraig was made of sterner stuff. "I expect to see the both of you in church tomorrow," he said. His Irish eyes twinkled as he added, "Wide awake."

Candy and Benj took their leave, with Candy waiting in her car for us.

Which left us alone with Anthony.

He too held a business envelope—a thick manila one, well-stuffed. Leah and I both raised our eyebrows.

He handed me the envelope. It contained a check to me for five grand. It also contained...

"Plane tickets to Rome, round trip, open-ended return," he said. "After all, you're both now traveling on a Vatican City diplomatic passport. You leave this coming Wednesday. I'm sure you'll figure out something to do while you're there. History *and* archeology. There are also papers for full medical insurance, now for the two of you... and for children to be added. It expires when you file for

Social Security. Eric, Leah...good luck, and I give my blessings to you."

Tears formed again as we got into Candy's old Chevy.

We had not gone more than four blocks when I realized that, in order to receive Anthony's envelope, I had laid down the one from Addison on the desk. Candy wheeled around and we sped back to the Foundry.

...it wasn't there. The Foundry wasn't there!

The hair salon directly abutted the restaurant. There was nothing in between. No Foundry. No office. No sign above the door. Nothing.

Shocked numb, we stood staring.

A young woman emerged from the hair salon, and aimed herself directly at us. She was holding Addison's envelope, or a very good approximation. It appeared to be sealed.

"He said to give you this," said the woman.

"Wh-who?" asked Leah.

"I don't know. I've never seen him before. But he described you two perfectly."

I was lost in a maze. "But...but there was a shop here, an office, between you and the restaurant..."

She shook her head. "Not as long as I've been working here, and that's what, fifteen years?"

I heard Leah gasp. My own words came raggedly. "Thank," I said. "All right, thank you."

"No problem," said the woman. She looked at Leah. "Anytime you want a new look."

"I'll stop by," Leah promised, her stunned tone empty.

Alone again, with Candy waiting in awe and puzzlement in the Chevy, we stared at the juncture between the salon and the restaurant, where the Foundry had been. There was—there could be—only one explanation for all that had transpired since the day I first showed up for work.

I got down on my knees on the sidewalk, and Leah with me. Her hand found mine. I now knew who Anthony really was. I had been right with my earlier thoughts. For reasons that were ineffable, God had created the role of Anthony for Himself; in effect, He was my, our, Burning Bush.

"This was all for us," I whispered. "To find each other. To bring us together. Leah, this was meant to be."

"Yes," she breathed. "I understand. I understand now." Her voice softened even further as she uttered a prayer. "Please keep us on the path, wherever it is Your Will to lead us, and give us the light to see it by."

"Amen."

Tears of joy and relief and love illuminated her face as she turned to me and said, "Let's go home, my husband."

About the Author:

The author is a retired U.S. Army translator now living in New Mexico, having moved there from Iowa in 2020 after his wife of 34 years passed. Specializing in science fiction, fantasy, and paranormal stories, he has written numerous novels, novellas, and short stories under his legal name, including the Bombay Sapphire superheroine series for Pro Se Press.

His Baptismal name is Tobias—therefore Toby—and he writes of religious theme under that name, including this present novel. He is currently working on a series of short stories until the title of *At the Hour of Our Death*. He does note that some of his Catholic beliefs are starting to seep into his other stories, to which his Guardian Angel has said, "It's about time!"